DEFINING EXCELLENCE
CULTURALLY RESPONSIVE TEACHING FOR 21ST CENTURY LEARNERS
by
Evelyn Rothstein, Maryanne Maisano, Massimo Marini

Constructive principles address learning as an individual process as well as a group or social process. Our own slogan is "Everyone knows something that someone else doesn't know" and it is this statement that permits all of us to learn from each other. In addition, this individualized self-knowledge, when tapped into in the classroom, can be the most enriching part of group learning. The concept of each individual's personal knowledge leads to the constructivist principles that state:

The purpose of learning is to construct meaning, not just memorize the "right" answer or state someone else's meaning.

With this principle accepted and posted in the classroom, we can begin the school year with each student from the primary grades through high school, making or writing a Metacognition Statement (Rothstein, Rothstein & Lauber 2007) and sharing it with classmates.

Copyright Evelyn Rothstein Learning Strategies ©2014 All rights reserved

All rights reserved. When forms and sample documents are included, their use is authorized only by educators, local school sites, and/or noncommercial or nonprofit entities who have purchased the book. Except for that usage, no part of this book may be reproduced or utilized in any form or by any means, electronic or mechanical, including photocopying, recording, or by any information storage and retrieval system, without permission in writing from the publisher.

ISBN 978-0-578-10957-2

THE BOOK

About the Authors

Evelyn Rothstein, Maryanne Maisano, Massimo Marini

Cover Illustration By Nicole Fuster

Preface – Defining Excellence

Introduction

Contents

Hallmarks of Excellence

- Responding to the Cultures of the Classroom
- Epochs of Change
- Student-Centered Teaching & Learning
- Individualizing Curriculum & Instruction Matched to the Needs, Talents, and Interests of ALL Learners
- Shared Vision & Commitment by All Stakeholders— Administration, Educators, Parents & Caregivers, Students & All Self-Directed Learners

Bibliography

Ancillary Materials

Dedication

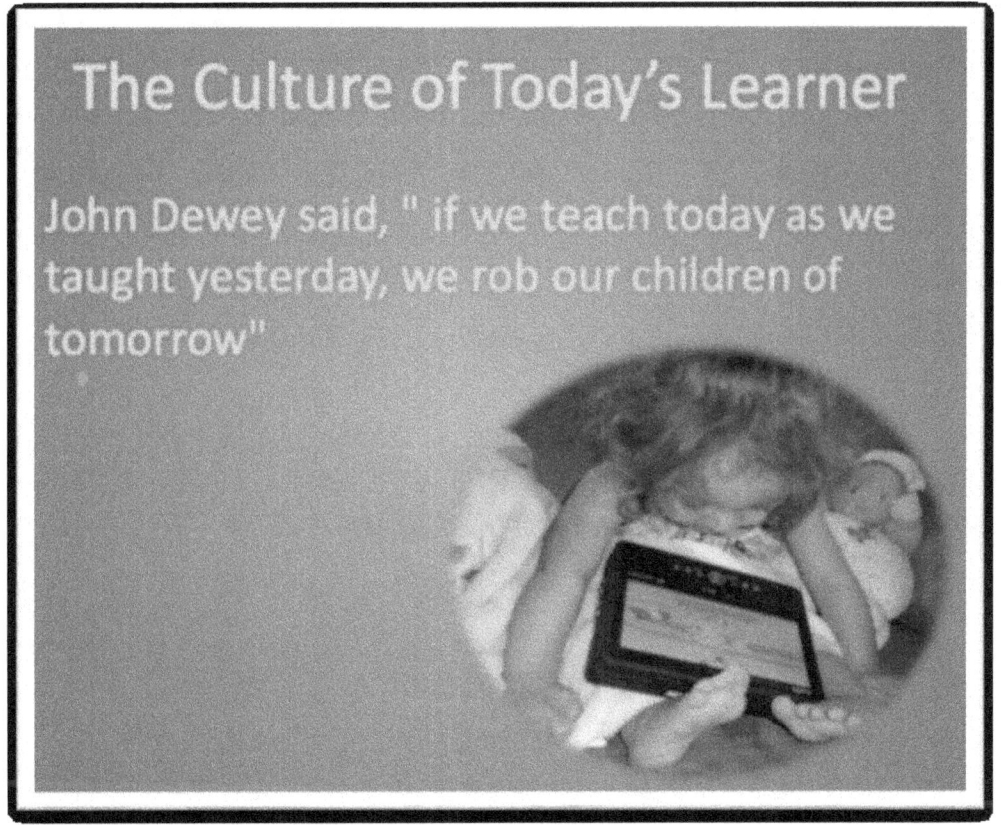

*Our book is dedicated to Arianna and Our Children & Grandchildren,
Learners of the 21st Century! Thank you for reminding us of what
DEFINING EXCELLENCE is all about and why we need to be Culturally Responsive
Educators!*

This book is testimony to the infinite possibilities of how the powerful new genres of 21st century literacy and technology can merge three authors across America to create a model of continuous professional development for ***DEFINING EXCELLENCE: Culturally Responsive Teaching for 21st Century Learners***.

From the Authors-

Maryanne

"Evelyn, it started with a professional development workshop over twenty years ago for making students better writers. I watched in awe at how developmentally appropriate strategies combined with culturally responsive teaching practices, allowed ALL students to be successful, intelligent, and valuable assets to school culture. You became my dearest friend, mentor, and beacon, showing me what IS important in the life of a self-directed learner. You are the source of light that guided me home to understand how it is possible in life as a wife, mother, and educator to do it all for the love of learning. We have reached incredible heights together and together will continue to model excellence for those we love.

Massimo, you are my childhood friend who through the years of familial ties brought us closer together. Now, your family and mine are part of the reason you and I have come to intellectually join our creative talents and provide quality education to those entrusted in our care. You are responsible for introducing me to the immersive world environment in order for me to better serve my students.

Evelyn

I respond to my friend--my dear inspirational friend—Maryanne with deepest thanks for the honor of being her mentor and then for the privilege of working with her side by side in this and all our other endeavors. We are bonded in many ways, with our love for education being the glue. Some twenty years ago, when she was a first-grade teacher in Florida and I came to her school as a New York consultant, we immediately knew we were a team. I had already seen many teachers teach, but the moment I walked into Maryanne's first grade classroom, I knew I was seeing the best.

So I asked myself, "What could I offer to the best?" And as we worked together, the answer unfolded. Maryanne had the intuition and talent to set up a classroom environment that would engage every child in wanting to learn and in enjoying every moment of that learning. Every child would be given the same opportunity to learn about art and music and story and numbers and language at the deepest levels. Every child had the gift for learning. No child was left out

And in this acknowledgement, I want to thank Dr. Robert L. Allen, my advisor and mentor from Teachers College who insisted that I learn about the English language deeply and ACCURATELY—What a gift!

Of course, there are also all the teachers-- hundreds-- who listened to me and liked what I said. What could be a greater tribute?

And then, there are the hundreds and hundreds of children whose classroom I visited, who also listened to me, and often laughed at all the funny statements and jokes that we get from our gift of language. From all these children, I received my own cultural education as they shared their heritages and stories and problems and successes.

Massimo

It seems that for every summit that I have achieved, I have had the inspiration and support from incredible women. So I use this moment to honor them and share how they led me to where I am today.

First, there is my mother Antonia, who came to this country reluctantly in 1956, kicking and screaming at my father's decision and hasn't stopped to this day. This strong willed woman taught me: "You work for what you want. No one owes you anything." At 86 she is still tending the garden and stomping the grapes with her feet. An amazing woman!

Dr. Evelyn Rothstein:

I am in awe of this woman. Since our first meeting, no one has held me both intellectually spellbound and on the edge of laughter simultaneously as Dr. Evelyn. Her depth of knowledge and passion for teaching has made it a joy and a learning experience at every meeting.

Dr. Maryanne Maisano:

In a chance meeting at a family function I reunited with my childhood friend Maryanne. While others were eating and dancing, we discovered we had both been working independently on virtual environments and decided to continue the conversation which began as an experiment that would lead hundreds of students receiving Professional Development into a virtual setting.

I thank Dr. Maryanne for reawakening the spark in teaching that was starting to dim and for offering this opportunity to take our work to a larger audience of students.

My wife, Mary:

None of my current work would be possible without the support of my wife. She is amused at my activities in the virtual world and teases me when she tells the children not to bother me as I am playing with my "Imaginary Friends".

She has given me the loving and supportive environment that is needed when exploring the new and unknown, whether I am taking classes, going to conventions, or attending the necessary meetings in person or virtually to work on this book. Mary's faith has encouraged me to tackle opportunities I might have allowed to pass me by.

About the Authors...

Maryanne Maisano began her educational career in the classroom, teaching all grades from primary to secondary, while formulating and developing her philosophy on student-centered teaching and learning. The student is always the focus and it is the student's strengths and interests that must drive the curriculum. Recognizing the value of this concept in her classroom teaching, Maryanne decided to open her own school, *The South Florida Academy of Learning,* to further test and expand her philosophy which became a hallmark of focusing on the students' strengths, interests, and needs. This endeavor led her to writing her dissertation on *A Work Of A.R.T.— Accountability, Responsibility and Teamwork—A Cross-Cultural Model for Individualizing Instruction.* Maryanne has been a Professor of Education at the University of North Carolina Pembroke, where she broke new ground in teacher education through technology and particularly through *Second Life*, a Virtual Immersive Learning Program that has built-in capabilities to create and facilitate culturally responsive instruction and learning. Her research led her to develop an immersive world environment specifically for teacher training. Student teachers have the opportunity to dispel trepidation of classroom teaching as a result of virtual practice in much the same way a pilot simulates flight before having souls on an aircraft. This work has led her to Keynote and Distinguished Speaker Series engagements across the globe from Vancouver BC, the US, Czech Republic, Finland, Spain and Italy.

 *Evelyn Rothstein* has been a classroom teacher, reading specialist, and an educational consultant for many years. She has her doctorate from Teachers College, Columbia University in Psycholinguistics, with her Masters Degree in Speech and Audiology and a Bachelors Degree in Education, both from The City University of New York. She began her teaching in the New York City schools, first as a third grade teacher and then in a fifth grade class. When she moved to the town of Nyack in New York State, she entered that Nyack Public Schools and moved into teaching reading. Several years later, Evelyn received a fellowship from Teachers College to do research on beginning reading. She would now work in other people's classes and move into the field of professional development and consulting. After the *Beginning Reading Project*, she became an advisor for the *Triple T Project (Training of Teacher Trainers)* at the City College of New York. While working independently, she also served with the *National Urban Alliance* for twelve years, an organization dedicated to under-served youth, mainly in inner-city environments.

In her life as a consultant, she has had the privilege of making presentations to educators across the United States and in France, Spain, Turkey, and Finland, focusing on the value and importance of language and language instruction as essential to school learning. Her three most recent publications—*Writing As Learning, Write for Mathematics*, and *English Grammar Instruction --That Works* (Corwin Press)—have provided teachers with instructional concepts and strategies that can elevate literacy to the highest possible learning levels.

Language is Evelyn's passion and comes from the belief that the role of the school is to give students the tools of learning, of which the major tool is communication. Now, with advent of computer technology, students can have extensive access to language, language research, and direct communication with speakers of other languages through the growing power of simultaneous translations and visualized contact with students of diverse cultures beyond the classroom.

She is also the author of six children's books based on the history of her family: *My Great Grandma Clara, My Great Grandpa Dave, Dave the Boxer, Clara Becomes a Citizen, Dave Learns Spanish,* and *Clara's Great War (*Marble House Editions*)*.

Massimo Marini never expected to be a teacher. In fact he was a corporate and social video producer for many years and developed training videos for clients such as Chase Manhattan Bank, Beneficial Finance, Exxon and Public Service Electric and Gas (PSE&G). During one video production for PSE&G, Massimo was taping a classroom presentation on energy generation and conservation and was fascinated by the children's engagement with the subject. He learned that they were in need of additional part time facilitators and offered to join them. And so the love affair with the classroom began.

Currently, a Middle School teacher in Hackensack New Jersey, Massimo teaches TV Production to grades 5-8 and produces a daily live morning news show in their TV studio. The children announce the news, operate all the equipment, and prepare the script for the teleprompter. He is proudest of the fact that he needs only to open the door and get out of their way. The students do the rest.

Massimo received his Communications BA and MA at William Paterson University and is currently completing an MA in Educational Technology.

Preface---Defining Excellence

Moving Beyond the Ordinary

Who could possibly oppose promoting an excellent education? In fact, we create an oxymoron with the words "poor education" since *education* means" to lead out" and supposedly to a better place. So why do we need to put the word *excellent* before education? Part of the answer comes with changing times. What might have served as excellent in one era no longer works as well in another time. Certainly a Greek and Roman classical education, while noble and uplifting for many of the Founders of America, seems to be passé, or at best, quaint, except for the few who are still attracted to the "classics."

But now in the 21st century, we refer to 21st century learners as a new breed of students, on the cusp of a technology that seems to hold no limits as we ponder what will be the education of today's ten-year old child ten years from now when this child is in college? Unlike almost any era that has preceded, the future is already here and moving at the metaphoric speed of light. So what are we to do?

As educators, in the field of education for a multiple of years, we hope to present the perspectives of our experiences as a basis for looking into the future, combined with the wisdom and knowledge that has already been accumulated by the vast number of educators, writers, and other scholars whose practices and words were always predictive of excellence. We are also including specific strategies—both in this book and with ongoing related digital media and on-line resources.

So we hope you, our readers and those entrusted in your care, can experience how we DEFINE *EXCELLENCE* which we believe results from cultural responsiveness, technological advances in our lives, and a focus on child/student-centered teaching and learning. If we are driven by the needs, talents and interests of our children we cannot help but keep our eye on the future and with this philosophy we will not fail our students.

...From Maryanne, Evelyn, and Massimo

Introduction

We have focused this book on key concepts that are essential to defining excellence in education and have provided strategies and activities that we believe support and enhance excellence when fully implemented. These concepts are:

Responding to the Cultures of the Technological Classroom in the 21st Century

Epochs of Change

Student-Centered Teaching and Learning

Individualizing Curriculum & Instruction Matched to the Needs, Talents, and Interests of ALL Learners

Shared Vision & Commitment by All Stakeholders —Self-directed Learners & Students, Parents & Caregivers, Educators & Administrators

The authors of this book believe that teachers require continuous professional development to maintain excellence, particularly as technology continues to evolve and expand as a major learning and teaching tool. Every teacher will be expected to keep up with the students in this technological advance and adventure, which clearly is a monumental challenge. With this challenge in mind, we have tried to prepare this book and its *ancillary features* as a growing product that you, as an educator, will not want to put away on the shelf, but will refer to and use as the major reference for educating your students. We will be open to your comments and suggestions and in this digital time of rapid transmission, we want to hear from you and we dedicate ourselves to responding and being responsive. Below we have outlined the five chapters, each of which is *layered* with sub-parts.

Chapter 1: Responding to the Cultures of the Technological Classroom

Cultures can only realize their further richness by honoring other traditions. Daisaku Ikeda – Japanese Peace Activist and Buddhist Leader, 1928. http://www.daisakuikeda.org/ retrieved November 10, 2013)

The three of us believe that for excellence to exist in current education, we must respond to what we believe are the "cultures" of the **technological classroom**. Whether we personally seek out cultural diversity or hold ourselves aloof from those we perceive as different, the technological advances already in effect will put us in contact with people we may never have imagined meeting and not just "meeting" but exchanging knowledge, ideas, and the inclusiveness of our different cultures. Already, the language barriers on the computer are crumbling so that students in Beijing will be talking to students in Chicago through *Skype, Voice Threads, Google Translation*, and who knows what else.

In this 21st century we have entered the **digital age for global communication**. Every day we need to learn a new computer program, a new filmmaking system, a new way to communicate, and more that is new and newer. With this demand, we have an essential question:

> **How can classroom teachers meet this challenge—a two-fold challenge that all of us educators must face when many of their young students are so far ahead digitally, while other students—those on the divide of poorer—only have access to the computers and digital equipment in their schools, much of which is already seriously outmoded?**

In addition, we must also focus on the plurality of the word *culture*. For example, there is youth culture, social culture, and ethnic culture, among other cultures. The word itself has other meanings such as references to behaviors, beliefs, and characteristics. Every person is like a Venn diagram, sharing a common culture, yet maintaining her or his own cultural uniqueness.

We also must know what teachers must be culturally responsive to and we need to make technology an integral part of these cultures. All of us past a certain age cannot know what our youth and children already know about computers, nor can we even try to keep track of who they are "talking" to and what they are learning. And as educators, we must be on an immediate search for the technological knowledge that is still in the "laboratories."

We refer to CULTURE in its broadest sense, following in part from the five aspects of culture stated in the Random House Webster's Unabridged Dictionary (1999). At least five of these aspects can result in the formation of a culturally responsive curriculum. We therefore devote the first chapter, to the concept of cultural responsiveness for 21st century learners, which we have integrated with student activities. Included are:

- Universals of Culture and Cultures in Our Classrooms
- The *Planning Wheel* as One Model for Culturally Responsive Teaching
- Culture and Language –"Prestigious vs. Non-Prestigious"
- The Literature of Culture
- Culture and Spirituality
- Mapping Cultural Universals
- The Family As Culture
- All Cultures Educate

Chapter 2: Epochs of Change

The ordinary 'horseless-carriage' is at present a luxury for the wealthy; and although the price will probably fall in the future, it will never, of course, come into as common use as the bicycle. –Anonymous

The history of humans is the history of change. Transportation by foot was changed with the invention of the wheel and the domestication of animals. Hunting and gathering fell behind with the advent of agriculture. The invention of writing systems resulted in schools. And so forth. These epochal changes always caused human adaptation and here we are being pushed to change in ways that are only barely foreseen, but are already on the horizon. Understanding epochs of change is our current history, that is, knowing what went before in order to imagine what is coming ahead. In this chapter, students are given the opportunity to study the history of change and become the predictors of the future. The availability of the Internet and new research programs will help students efficiently and effectively find historic information that can readily be kept up to date.

In chapter two we present these segments by focusing on *Epochs of Change and Educational Implications*

- The Wheel for Distance Transportation and Shared Information
- Agriculture for Changing Societies from Hunters/Gatherers to Permanent Dwellers
- Alphabets and Iconic Symbols to Keep Records and Share Ideas
- Weaponry and Its Effect on Technology
- Inventions to Connect and Expand Knowledge – Electricity, Microscopes, Telescopes, and others to come
- Horseless Locomotions to Move Us With Great Speed – Cars, Airplanes, Rockets
- Electronics for a Digital Age to Create Global Communication

Chapter 3: Student-Centered Teaching & Learning

Teaching is fundamentally about creating the pedagogical, social, and ethical conditions under which students agree to take charge of their own learning, individually and collectively.

Richard F. Elmore, Education for Judgment: The Artistry of Discussion Leadership, www.gse.harvard.edu/faculty_research (retrieved November 10, 2013),

With students learning and creating new technologies, our focus for the 21st century classroom is *Student-Centered Teaching and Learning*. We have selected five principles related to the concept of *student-centered* in contrast to "group" centered such as homogenous vs. heterogeneous, or low groups or high groups. While we have always believed in the idea of student-centered teaching and learning, this aspect is now essential for developing a technology environment where previous "classroom skills" are at times becoming secondary to technological skills. Homogenous grouping and age-related grouping will have new meanings in a technological classroom and school. Our five principles of student-centered teaching and learning therefore require:

- Developing a Variety of Models for All Learners
- Expanding Learning Goals
- Technological Curriculum for Now and the Future
- Finding Your Niche, Building Your Interests
- Connecting to Diversity Real and Virtual

Chapter 4: Individualizing Curriculum & Instruction Matched to the Needs, Talents, and Interests of ALL Learners

No child will be left behind if the individual learning needs of the child are met. (Hamby. 1989). www.ericdigests.org/pre-9219/risk.htm (retrieved November 10, 2013)

With the current heavy emphasis on testing and the comparing scores of low-achieving students with high-achieving students, we have neglected or masked the wonderful individuality and learning diversities of our students. What has happened to our artists and musicians or to our cartoonists, humorists, and poets, or the actors and athletes, all of whom bring other forms of diversity to our classroom? Have we heard the languages of our bilingual or multilingual students, sang their songs, tasted their food, and exchanged stories? Are we directly in touch with people from other cultures and from great distances?

With the expansion of technology for effective teaching and learning, we now have the means for individualizing and matching that will allow schools and teachers to:

- Create dynamic, integrated curriculum in all subject areas
- Foster innovative, energetic, and inspirational work
- Design service learning and leadership opportunities
- Develop characteristics and attributes for responsible global citizenship
- Offer opportunity for introductions to languages and cultures to better facilitate relationships world-wide
- Promote stewardship of the Earth and respect for our natural environment

Chapter 5: Shared Vision & Commitment by All Stakeholders – Students, Parents, Teachers, and Administrators

A shared vision, with technology as a partner, may be difficult to achieve because it means openness, cooperation, listening to all sides, and the putting aside of competitiveness. This is the same type of shared vision that countries and communities need to build, united by their collective strengths and avoiding the separation and segregation that leads to economic and social divisiveness. Responding to the cultures of the classroom, having student-centered teaching and learning, and individualizing curriculum and instruction must be in place or, at least in progress, for the shared vision to work. The stakeholders, therefore, have a commitment to foster:

- socio-cultural awareness and positive attitudes toward diverse backgrounds
- curriculum change to meet social, economic, and technological changes
- pride in the talents and accomplishment of all the students
- strengthening of the educational goals for the benefit of the total community
- belief in the value of social, economic, and technological changes
- opportunity for continuous professional development and support systems for those who engage in defining excellence in education

With so many books and articles and dissertations on education, what could we add that's new and meaningful? As the world of technology orbits around us and the global population builds new pathways of communication, our students are in a new planet where desks, writing implements, lectures, departmentalized classes, and other memories of our own education are already in the archives. So looking ahead, as best as we can, we set forth our vision and proposals for living in the speed of the 21st century. Throughout this book, we have noted the ancillary materials that will allow you to expand your teaching and classroom activities and we urge you to make use of them.

Epilogue – The Future – It's With Us Everyday
We have to implement new ideas quickly, because in a short time we're likely to be outmoded!

FIGURES BY CHAPTER

Chapter 1

- The Planning Wheel
- Taxonomies of First Names, Places of Birth & Favorite Foods
- Country Profile
- Cultural Group Profile
- Taxonomy of Women Mathematicians
- Taxonomy of Mathematicians of the African Diaspora
- Taxonomy of Mathematicians of Latino/Latina Heritage
- Framed Sentences for Mathematicians of Magnitude
- Friendly to Formal
- Formal to Friendly
- Frame for Telling About a Book With a Cultural Theme
- Taxonomy of Spiritual Celebrations, Festivities, or Holidays
- Profile of a Holiday, Celebration, or Festival
- Taxonomy of World-Wide Cultural Groups
- Cultural Group Profile (2)
- Family Members in Hebrew
- Family Relations of the Hopi Tribe
- Family Relationships in Vietnam
- Proverbs From the Islamic World
- Chants, Clapping Games, and Jump Rope Rhymes
- American Geography Through Songs

Chapter 2

- Wheels and Vehicles in Our Lives
- Metacognition Frame of a Wheeled Vehicle
- The Wheel in Expanding Human Knowledge
- Domesticated Animals
- Defining Format – What Is a Llama?
- Taxonomy of Domesticated Animals in Five Languages
- Regions Where Wheat and Rice are Grown
- Taxonomy of Grains for Consumption
- Defining Format for a Specific Grain
- Recipe for Making Tortillas

- The Greek Alphabet
- Letters of the Cyrillic (Russian) Alphabet
- Letters of the Hebrew Alphabet
- The Arabic Alphabet
- Language Profile
- The Cherokee Syllabary
- Letters in Braille
- The Manual Alphabet
- Chronology of Weapons
- Research a Weapon
- How Coyote Stole Fire
- What is a Myth?
- Frame for Writing a Myth
- Taxonomy of Scientists and Inventors Related to Electricity
- Eponyms of Spark
- Sampling of Biologists and Astronomers
- Personifications and Interactions – Biologist to Astronomer and Vice-Versa
- Who's Who in the Digital Story
- Person of Accomplishment Frame

Chapter 3

- Letters Between Abigail Adams and John Adams
- Harriet Tubman Texts Sojourner Truth
- Writing What You Know About to a Friend and Classmate
- Dialogue Between Little Red Riding Hood and Snow White
- An English Only Trip Through America
- Dialogue Between an Earthling and a Martian on Expanded Notation
- Dialogue Between an Earthling and a Martian on Mathematical Terms
- Dialogue Between an Earthling and a Martian on "What is Algebra?"
- Varieties of Communicating from One Word to Many
- Seeing the Big Picture Through Morphology
- Building a Noun Department Store
- Cities and Their Rivers
- Definition of a Colony

- Definition of a Fable
- Definition of a Legend
- Definition of a Folk Tale
- Definition of a Myth
- Characteristics of Four Literary Genres
- What We Know That We Know
- Chronology of Weapons
- Research a Weapon

Chapter 4
- Three Citations from the Finnish Educational System
- Survey of Organization for Economic Cooperation and Development
- Taxonomy of Students' Needs, Talents, Qualities, and Interests
- Writing About One of Your Interests
- A Frame About Your Teacher and You
- A Personal Profile
- My Dream
- Sharing Your Knowledge
- What's So Funny?
- Body Language
- Oxymora
- Eponyms
- Colorful Words and Phrases
- Affixes Awry
- Comedic Characters
- Comedic Characters to Create a Character

Chapter 5
- Teachers, Grades, Subjects, Interests, and Talents
- Teacher Collaboration Models
- Qualities and Attributes of a Good Teacher
- Six Hours of Instruction in a Five-Hour Day
- Looking Back
- Memory Highlights
- Down Memory Lane

- My Accomplishments From Then to Now
- Feelings
- I Have a Dream
- Ten Years From Now
- "I Can…"

Hallmarks of Excellence

What we want is to see is the child in pursuit of knowledge, and not knowledge in pursuit of the child.-- George Bernard Shaw

The larger the island of knowledge, the longer the shoreline of wonder.-- Ralph M. Sockman

The whole world opened to me when I learned to read.-- Mary McLeod Bethune

No problem can be solved by the same consciousness that created it. We need to see the world anew.' Albert Einstein

The first people had the questions, and they were free. The second people had answers, and they became enslaved. Wind Eagle Modern Indian Medicine Woman

I don't know what the future may hold, but I know who holds the future.-- Ralph Abernathy

One can never consent to creep when one feels the compulsion to soar. Helen Keller

It is today we must create the world of the future. Eleanor Roosevelt

Do not go where the path may lead; go instead where there is no path and leave a trail. Ralph Waldo Emerson

CHAPTER ONE
RESPONDING TO THE CULTURES OF THE TECHNOLOGICAL CLASSROOM

---

cul·ture (adapted from Random House Webster's Unabridged Dictionary, 1998)

1. the sum total of ways of living built up by a group of human beings and transmitted from one generation to another

2. the behaviors and beliefs characteristic of a particular social, ethnic, or age group: *the youth culture; the drug culture.*

3. the development or improvement of the mind by education or training

4. the quality in a person or society that arises from a concern for what is regarded as excellent in arts, letters, manners, scholarly pursuits, etc.

5. a particular form or stage of civilization, as that of a certain nation or period: *Greek culture.*

The Universals of Culture and Cultures in Our Classroom

The role of culture reaches beyond racial and ethnic groups....(Sowell, 1998, x)

Culture -- Definition 1
– The sum total of ways of living built up by a group of human beings and transmitted from one generation to another.

This first definition of culture, from the *Webster Random House Dictionary (1998)*, focuses on what we see as universals, meaning that all humans share a set of behaviors that unites us as humans. As we metaphorically look across the world and remove pre-judgments, we observe these aspects of all humanity regardless of geography or racial and ethnic attributes. To illustrate this unity of humanity we present the following:

> **THE UNIVERSALS OF CULTURE**
> **ALL CULTURES LIVE IN SOME ARRANGEMENT OF FAMILY UNITS**
> **ALL CULTURES EDUCATE THEIR CHILDREN IN THE WAYS OR MORES OF THEIR CULTURE**
> **ALL CULTURES SPEAK A HIGHLY DEVELOPED COMPLEX LANGUAGE**
> **ALL CULTURES KNOW SOMETHING THAT OTHER CULTURES DON'T KNOW**
> **ALL CULTURES HAVE CELEBRATIONS, FESTIVITIES, MUSIC, AND MOURNING**
> **ALL CULTURES HAVE A SPIRITUAL SENSE CONNECTED TO A SENSE OF WONDERMENT OF THE WORLD**

There are times when we overlook or negate these aspects of culture because they don't match what we think of as "our" cultures and we tend to focus on the differences in contrast to the similarities. For example, in the Australian film, *Rabbit Proof Fence* (2002), we see Aborigine mothers who have given birth to "mixed-breed children," children who are now considered inferior and dangerous to the white population. The Australian government believes that the way to "save" these children is to breed them with "white mates" where they will eventually absorb the culture of the white population. The plan is to kidnap the "mixed-breed" children "for their own good".

We may shudder at such an idea, but what this deeply emotional film shows is how three of the kidnapped children—girls—use their knowledge to escape their captives and find their way back, 1500 miles from their home, following the path of a rabbit proof fence that the Australian farmers have constructed to keep out the flood of rabbits invading their farms. Molly, 12 years old, and the oldest of the three siblings, tries to lead her sisters home to the mother and family members she loves and yearns for. She consoles her younger sisters in the Aborigine language that allows her to express everything she needs to say. She knows how to find birds' eggs for food and how to cover her tracks by removing her shoes and wearing only her socks. At home, as the family mourns for the loss of their children, everyone in the community "prays" with sorrow and hope. When only two of the sisters return home, because one of them was re-kidnapped, the village celebrates and mourns—of course.

Expanding Our Definition of Culture in A Digital Age

Even our definition of culture must expand when we realize the effects of the technological advances we have experienced and the ones to come. Whether we are digital immigrants or are digital natives (Prensky, 2001) as our students are, the concept of culture extends well beyond our homes, neighborhoods, states, countries and includes the idea that we can connect with anyone, anytime, anywhere. This is a cultural unity unlike any the world has ever seen. Even if we personally hold ourselves aloof from those we perceive as different, the technological advances already in effect can put us in contact with people we may never have imagined meeting and not just "meeting" but exchanging knowledge, ideas, and the inclusiveness of our different cultures. Already, the language barriers on the computer are crumbling so that students and teachers in Beijing are talking to students and teachers in Chicago through *Skype, Voice Threads, Google Translation*, and more to come.

We must visualize what a culturally responsive classroom looks like and which reflects the instructional focus. Gay (2000) defines culturally responsive teaching as using cultural knowledge, prior experiences, and performance styles to make learning more effective. With students learning and creating new technologies, the focus for the 21st century classroom must be *Student-Centered Teaching and Learning*, in contrast to "group" centered such as homogenous vs. heterogeneous, low group or high groups, achievers or non-achievers. Grouping of all types will have new meanings in a digital classroom. In addition, culturally responsive teaching is student-centered teaching which means that we match curriculum and instruction to the needs, talents and interests of all learners. Knowing whom we teach first, before knowing what we teach, establishes a frame of reference for the work in the classroom. When we know the students, the blue print for serving them becomes clear. The way to do this includes any and all appropriate methods for identifying learning styles and more clinical pre-assessments of strengths and weaknesses, but really starts as simple as recognizing them, learning their names, and listening to what they know and what they want to know. By being student centered you create autonomy for every student and recognize that the students bring value and can contribute to the learning in the classroom. One specific aspect of this principle is *drawing on and including the traditions and heritages of student diversity and diversities for living in a global society.*

To implement this plan, we introduce a powerful instructional strategy based on the work of Evelyn Rothstein (2007, 2009). *The Planning Wheel,* Figure 1.1 provides a framework for designing instruction across all disciplines that is the necessary requisite to insure learning for all students.

The Planning Wheel, Figure 1.1 from *Writing As Learning* (2007) is a model for teaching that uses the "topic" to develop in-depth, high-level learning. The figure of the Planning Wheel graphically illustrates the centrality of the topic – what the students are studying—and twelve strategies for the student to develop in-depth knowledge of that topic. The strategies are not organized by sequence of importance, but are placed on the wheel equally to represent the importance of each strategies. The strategies are designed to build "fluency, organization, and thinking skills" by having the students learn the vocabulary related to the topic by creating *Taxonomies* (categories of terms that become the student's personal thesaurus) *Composing With Keywords* for speaking and writing about the topic, Metacognition for thinking and writing about the topic in an organized statement, and *Defining Format* to guide the student in creating clear, unambiguous definitions about the vocabulary specific to the topic. In addition, the student learns the vocabulary in-depth—meaning the students learn the *morphological* structure of words and their *etymology* or background history.

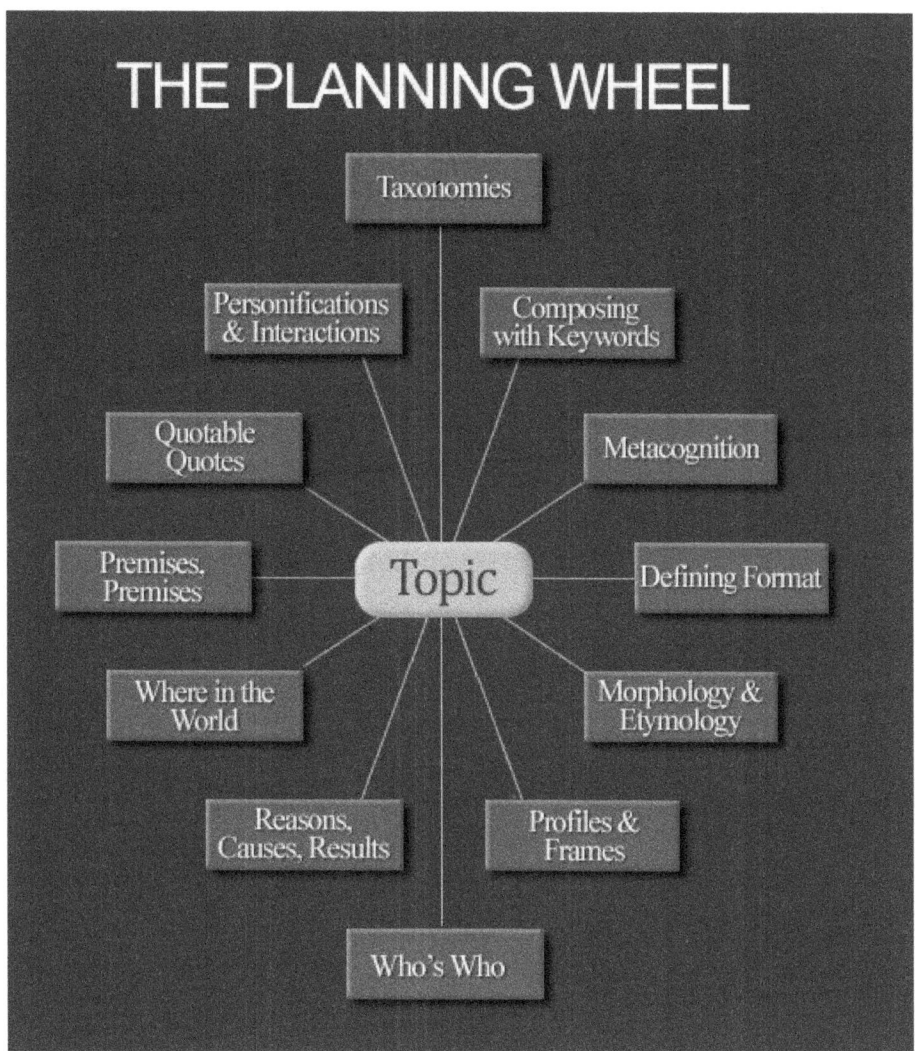

The second aspect of the Planning Wheel is to give the students guidance in organizing ideas and concepts. *Profiles and Frames* are templates for research and adding information and for guiding the student in the writing in various genres—science, mathematics, fiction, and other forms. And to include the cultural aspects of all learning or all topics, students must know *Who's Who*, meaning knowing the people who created the knowledge that we have inherited and that allows us to create new knowledge. Who are the other creators who form the basis of what we call our "curriculum? "Who's Who" is not only intrinsically interesting, but represents a cultural collage of the world. A compendium of "Mathematicians of Magnitude", for example, is a world list representing every continent and culture.

The strategy of *Where in the World* makes sure that every student knows that whatever we know came from some place, ex: pasteurization in France, the microscope from Holland, cotton goods from Egypt, and on and on with every culture contributing to the melting pots of products. *No topic can be without geography or people.*

The other strategies in the Planning Wheel—*Reasons, Causes, Results, Premises, Premises, Quotable Quotes,* and *Interactions and Personifications* continue to provide the students with the *tools* of good writing and communication, making them both knowledgeable and highly literate and capable of using the ever-expanding *tools* of a digital and technological world.

Start your culturally responsive instruction with Figures 1.2, *Taxonomies,*
Figure 1.3 *Country Profile,* Figure 1.4 *Cultural Group Profile* based on The Planning Wheel as illustrated in Writing As Learning (2007). These figures will introduce students to the concept of *Where in the World* (Writing as Learning, 2007)

Taxonomies

Begin by having students set up *Taxonomies* (Rothstein, Rothstein, & Lauber *Writing As Learning 2007*). Taxonomies in this context are ABC lists on specific topics to which all students contribute. Following is an example of student names illustrating the possible diversity in a classroom and serving as the starting point for students learning about their own background as well as the background of their classmates. Taxonomies are extremely useful in all subject areas because they insure that the students are directing the learning they need by creating the bank of vocabulary words that represent what they already know—prior knowledge—with all the things they need to know.

Figure 1.2 TAXONOMIES OF FIRST NAMES, PLACES OF BIRTH, & FAVORITE FOODS
(Example for your students)

	OUR FIRST NAMES		FAMILY PLACES OF BIRTH	FAMILY'S FAVORITE FOODS
A	Ahman	A	Albania, Armenia, Argentina	arroz con pollo
B	Brittany	B	Botswana, Bolivia, Brazil, Barbados, Bangladesh, Belgium	burrito, borscht, ban bao, blintzes, burritos
C	Chavis	C	Canada, Costa Rica, China	curried chicken, crepe, calzone
D	Desiree	D	Denmark, Dominican Republic	dabo kolo, dim sum
E	Elena	E	Ethiopia, El Salvador, Eritrea	eggs
F	Francesca	F	France, Finland	falafel
G	Gary	G	Guatemala, Greece, Grenada	gumbo
H	Hui-yu	H	Haiti, Hungary	hamburger, humus
I	Isabella	I	Italy, Israel, India, Iraq, Iran, Ireland	ice cream
J	Juan	J	Japan, Jordan, Jamaica	jambalaya
K	Ken'Ichi	K	Kenya	kreplach
L	Lazar	L	Laos, Lebanon	lo mein, maize
M	Musa	M	Mexico, Malta	moussaka
N	Nguyen	N	Nigeria, Norway, Netherlands	noodle kugel
O	Omar	O	Outer Mongolia	okra
P	Pierre	P	Poland, Portugal, Paraguay, Puerto Rico, Pakistan	pizza, pierogi, plaintain, paella
Q	Quaneisha	Q	Quebec	quiche
R	Reza	R	Russia, Rwanda, Rumania	roast chicken
S	Shaday	S	Surinam, South Africa, Somalia, Senegal, Saudi Arabia, Spain, Syria, Sweden, Switzerland, Singapore	sushi, sweet potato pie
T	Tanya	T	Taiwan, Trinidad	tapas
U	Umi	U	U.S.A., Uruguay, Ukraine, United Kingdom	ugali
V	Vladimir	V	Vietnam, Venezuela	veal paprika
W	Willie	W		waffles, won ton
X	Xenia	X		
Y,Z	Yonas, Zeena	Y	Yemen, Zimbabwe	yams

Where in the World

All too often, very little geography gets taught throughout the grades and when it is taught, it is generally limited to grade level curriculum. But in a culturally responsive environment, every grade, every class, and every subject matter and every content area has a geographic history and presents us with the glorious opportunity of sharing history and expanding our global knowledge. *Where in the World* offers a geographic point of reference for the content the students are learning, whether it be England because they are studying Shakespeare's plays, Greece because they are reading Homer's Odyssey or France because they are studying pasteurization and Louie Pasteur. We offer here two *Where in the World* strategies, Figure 1.3. Country Profile and Figure 1.4 Cultural Group Profile. Country Profile is a simple way to start students learning about a country that is interesting to them. Cultural Group Profile offers the students an organizing template for researching a topic and noting its important or meaningful details or characteristics.

Figure 1.3 COUNTRY PROFILE

COUNTRY PROFILE

Directions: Select a country you would like to know more about and complete the template below. When you have all the information, write a report about that country and share it with your classmates, friends, family, neighbors, and anyone else willing to listen and learn from you.

Name of Country _____ Country's Continent _____

Bordering countries _____

Bordering waters _____

Area of country _____

Country's population _____

Capital city _____

Major cities _____

Language(s) spoken _____

Colors of the flag _____

Name of currency _____

Important products _____

Form of government _____

Political divisions within country (ex. states, provinces) _____

Other information _____

Figure 1.4 CULTURAL GROUP PROFILE

CULTURAL GROUP PROFILE
Name of Group _____
Original Habitat _____
Major Means of Livelihood
Type(s) of Dwellings _____
Language(s) _____
Form(s) of Governance _____
Major Roles and Tasks of Women _____
Major Roles and Tasks of Men _____
Significant Beliefs _____
Current Life Style _____
Types of Food _____
Major Festivals or Festivities _____
Members of Accomplishment _____
Other Information _____

Who's Who-- So many schools teach subjects without its humanity, forgetting to include the *people of accomplishment* who have been at the forefront of discovery, research, and inventions that have provided us with subject area knowledge. Great mathematicians are rarely commented upon in mathematics textbooks, chemistry is often taught with little mention of the scientists who laboriously and creatively sorted out the "matter" that makes up our world, and rarely do we "circle the globe" for those women and men of diversity who have added to our knowledge and comfort.

As a starting point on *Who's Who*, we have included Taxonomies that can get students involved in researching mathematicians from around the world. We have also added Mathematicians of Magnitude from *Write for Mathematics* (Rothstein, Rothstein, & Lauber 2007). These Who's Who activities can be used not only by teachers of mathematics, but by every teacher who sees the value of linking "people" to learning. In addition, Who's Who can be adapted for science, social studies, language arts, and other areas. We present them in Figures 1.5, 1.6, 1.7 and 1.8. You can use the Taxonomies as is, or modify them by adding a country of origin for specific grades.

Figure 1.5 Taxonomy of Women Mathematicians (Add Others)

A	Agnesi, Andrews
B	Bacon, Bernstein
C	Cartwright, Chang
D	Duabechie, Dickerman
E	
F	Falconer
G	Germain, Granville
H	Hjagood, Herschel
I	
J	Janovskaja
K	Karp, Kupferberg
L	Lazar, Litivinova
M	Macintyre, Moufang
N	Nightingale, Noether
O	Oleinik, Owens
P	Pierce, Pless
Q	
R	Ragsdale, Robinson
S	Sodosky, Srinivasan
T	Theano, Turner
U	Uhlenbeck
V	Velez-Rodriguez. Vivian
W	Weiss, Wheeler
X	
Y	Young (Anna Irwin) Young (Lai-Sang
Z	

CHAPTER ONE: RESPONDING TO THE CULTURES OF THE TECHNOLOGICAL CLASSROOM

Figure 1.6 Taxonomy of Mathematicians of the African Diaspora--People of African birth who live in different parts of the world (Add the countries of origin and other names.)

A	Agboola, Asani
B	Blackwell
C	Chukwu
D	
E	Ekhaguerre
F	Farley
G	Gangbo
H	Hunt
I	
J	
K	
L	
M	Massey
N	
O	Okikiolu
P	Petters
Q	
R	Richards
S	
T	
U	
V	
W	Wilkins
X	
Y	
Z	

Figure 1.7 Taxonomy of Mathematicians of Latino/Latina Heritage (Add the countries of origin and other names)

A	Adem-Diaz de Leon
B	Banuelos
C	Calderon (Alberto)
D	
E	
F	Flores
G	Gatica
H	
I	Iovino
J	
K	
L	
M	Martinez (Cleopatria)
N	
O	Otero
P	
Q	
R	Rubio-Canabel
S	Saavedra
T	Torrejon
U	Uribe-Ahumada
V	Valdez (Linda)
W	
X	
Y	
Z	

Figure 1.8 FRAMED SENTENCES FOR MATHEMATICIANS OF MAGNITUDE

Directions: Use the following FRAME to write an information-bearing sentence about a Mathematician of Magnitude who contributed a major idea to the study of mathematics. There are five examples to help you get started. You can use this sentence FRAME for starting a biography or a project. The Internet can help you find information.

Starting Frame:

_____ *was/is* _____ *who*

_____.

1. Mohammed Al-Kwarizimi was a Muslim scholar who coined the word *algorithm* and contributed to the ideas of polynomials with an infinite number of terms.
2. Ilse Meitner was an Austrian-born nuclear physicist and mathematician who contributed numerous papers to quantum theory and was a member of the Swedish Nobel Institute and the Atomic Energy Commission.
3. Katherine Okikiolu, born in Nigeria and living in the United States, is a scientist and mathematician who has conducted innovative research in geometric analysis and has developed curricula in mathematics for students of all ages.
4. Stanislaw Ulam, a 20th century Swedish mathematician, worked on early computers and showed how simple structures such as squares and triangles could become extremely complex.
5. Lai-Sang Young, born in Hong Kong in 1952 and now living in the United States, is a professor of mathematics doing research on the mathematical theory of dynamical systems and is a winner of a Guggenheim Fellowship for distinguished achievement.

Teaching and learning requires the use of language. Language is part of culture. For better or worse we judge and are judged by the language we use. From an academic perspective we all too often stereotype one another's intellectual capacity or ability based on how they speak. By using the strategies and frames the planning wheel provides, we are able to celebrate the traditions and heritage of student diversity and diversities for living in a global society.

Culture and Language – Prestigious and Non-Prestigious

> **EVELYN BIERMAN ROTHSTEIN – TEACHER WITH A NEW YORK ACCENT**
>
> Many years ago when Evelyn entered the School of Education in the City College of New York, she was immediately assigned to Remedial Speech Class, with hundreds of other students, to **cure** her of her New York Accent. A team of speech experts from Michigan were hired, as prototypes of Henry Higgins, to change the speech sounds of all these students of Eastern European heritage, even if they were born in America and English was their first, and often only, language. Once again, Evelyn, along with others, was tested by these experts from Michigan and found to be failing in speech.
>
> She had: *diphtongalization, dentalization, r-lessness, and –ng click*, serious New York accent failings in comparison to the American standard exemplified by mid-western Americans.
>
> She was threatened with failure to receive a diploma and, therefore, there was no possibility of ever teaching in a middle-class New York City school. Only with intensive daily speech practice, and possible visits to the Midwest, would Evelyn get her diploma.
>
> Luckily, because of the heavy failure rate of the students with New York accents, City College rescinded this requirement just one year before Evelyn was scheduled to graduate.
>
> PS – Because of the continued persistence of this accent, she was not allowed to teach in a white, middle class school, but was assigned to an African-American school in Harlem. A life-changing experience for Evelyn for which she is ever grateful, thanks to her low prestigious New York accent.

Not everyone would agree that all people speak a highly complex language. In fact, many of us have been accustomed to separating language as "prestigious" and "non-prestigious", often assuming that languages labeled Creole, Patois, Ebonics, Cajun, or Gullah could not possibly be complex. And even if they are complex, they are certainly not considered prestigious!

Prestigious vs. Non-Prestigious	
French	Haitian
Italian	Sicilian
English	Ebonics
German	Yiddish
Castilian Spanish	Nicaraguan Spanish

What did you notice? On what basis did you make your decision? Did you base it all on complexity? Do the Navajos speak a less complex language than the Hopi? Or are such comparisons ridiculous? Our opinions of the quality of a language come from the viewpoints based on social status and economic power. All humans learn a NATIVE LANGUAGE, learn it YOUNG, and if there are no physical, mental, or emotional complications, learn it WELL. Understanding this concept of language, known as sociolinguistics, is essential to maintaining a culturally responsive classroom.

Some of us may be uncomfortable with such a broad acceptance of language. We ask: What about "academic language" vs. "street language". What about "correct" vs. "incorrect" Isn't my job as a teacher to "elevate my students' language"? The answers to these questions cannot be answered with a YES or NO, but with an understanding of each speaker's heritage and experience, always keeping in mind that we speak the language we have learned at home and/or in our community. We cannot speak a language we have never heard, nor do we easily learn a second language except when we are young and immersed in it, similar to our learning our first language (2003 Crystal, 1998 Delpit).

A very important aspect of language, which you should introduce to your students, is called *register*, which refers to the formalities or informalities of language (Rothstein &

Rothstein, 2009.) For example, we are likely to speak one way to a prospective employer in "formal" English, another way to a peer, using "conversational" English, and quite differently to a young child, using "baby" talk. Teenagers speak in different registers to other teenagers in contrast to how they speak to their parents (2001 Delpit).

An excellent strategy to make your students aware of different registers and gain practice in using them is to use *Personifications and Interactions* as illustrated in Figure 1.9 Friendly to Formal and Figure 1.10. Formal to Friendly. This strategy is particularly valuable in social studies and can also be used in science.

Figure 1.9 Friendly to Formal

> **EDMUND BURKE, MEMBER OF THE BRITISH PARLIAMENT WRITES TO BENJAMIN FRANKLIN**
>
> *You will notice immediately that the voice of this letter is very friendly. If the letter was going to be published in either a British or American newspaper, the voice might have to be different.*
>
> *Rewrite this letter for "publication."*
>
> Dear Ben,
>
> I hear that things in the Colonies are in pretty bad shape. We heard that a group of rascals dumped some of our good English tea into Boston harbor. Those guys acted a bit looney painting their faces and carrying on like a bunch of crazies. I can't believe that you colonists want to split from us Brits. As we say here, King George ain't that bad. He thinks he's some kind of big wheel who can boss the little guys around. But even kings kick the bucket (ya know), so just hang in. Get back to me and send my best to the wife and kiddies.   Your buddy, Ed

Figure 1.10 Formal to Friendly

ELIZABETH CADY STANTON, SUFFRAGIST WRITES TO SUSAN B. ANTHONY, SUFFRAGIST.

You will notice that Elizabeth Cady Stanton who is a friend of Susan B. Anthony is writing in a very formal style. Rewrite the letter so it's more friendly and personal.

Dear Miss Anthony:

News has just arrived that you have been placed on trial for attempting to vote and for advocating a Constitutional Amendment that would give the suffrage to women. You well know that the political establishment is vehemently opposed to such a radical concept of women voting, a right heretofore reserved for males.

Be assured, you have my unwavering support for your difficult endeavor. I am most hopeful that your trial ends in a verdict of not guilty and I shall continue to support you in this essential undertaking. Very cordially yours,

                                        Elizabeth Cady Stanton

The Literature of Culture

Fortunately, the language arts curriculum offers students stories and other literary items that introduce authors, cultural topics, and geographic locations that provide a more global and cultural perspective than the other subject areas. Often, however, the focuses in most language arts classrooms are likely to be more weighted to *"What is the story about?"* without in-depth information about the cultural aspects. Since one of the universals of culture is the human triad of celebrations, festivals, and mourning, the language arts classroom can naturally focus on culture, but we encourage anyone teaching in any subject area to become aware of the culture associated with your content and seek out literature to enhance your instruction.

We'd like to share the books published and illustrated by Elizabeth Uhlig who has focused on the genre of memoirs, most of which have cultural themes and naturally include the celebrations and festivals and also the losses that are part of life. We have selected a sampling of these books and refer you to the website www.marble-house-editions.com for more. At the end of this display is a Writing Frame, Figure 1.11, to guide students in sharing what they have learned from a cultural perspective. Included with the resources are lists of materials that can used to incorporate cultural literature into any subject area.

Clara Becomes a Citizen

Written by Evelyn Rothstein Illustrated by Elizabeth Uhlig

Marble House Editions, June 2009, ages 8-12

About the book: Clara came to America from Europe in 1920, but by the end of the 1930s she still had not become an American citizen. With work, marriage, and raising a family, there just wasn't time to study for the citizenship test. Now a war is starting in Europe and to be truly secure, Clara has got to get her naturalization papers. But how will she learn and remember everything for the test? It's a daunting task, but with her daughter's help, Clara is determined to pass.

Dave the Boxer by Evelyn Rothstein, illustrated by Elizabeth Uhlig

About the book: When Dave was fourteen, he began to visit a place called a Settlement House where boys and girls could play ping pong or checkers or do sports. One of the sports was boxing. Dave liked to watch boxing and began to wonder. "Maybe I can be a boxer. I like boxing and I think boxers make more money than newspaper boys or flower sellers or even working on a coal wagon." Dave, a young boy living in Old New York, needs to find a way to help support his family. After considering some of the everyday jobs on the Lower East Side, like selling newspapers or having a pushcart, Dave decides to try his hand at amateur boxing. This is a story about courage, determination, and self-acceptance.

Published by Marble House Editions, paperback, , July 2011For ages 8 through 14.

My Great Grandpa Dave Written by Evelyn Rothstein
Illustrated by Elizabeth Uhlig   Marble House Editions, May 2007,
Ages 8-12

> **About the book**: Dave is a young boy growing up in New York City about 100 years ago. When he is sent home from school by the school nurse at age seven, he goes to work to help his family and misses five years of school. With the help of his beloved sister Lena, who teaches him at home, Dave learns to read poetry, recites Shakespeare, and becomes a champion speller. This is the touching story of a boy and his sister, and their love for learning.

My Great Grandma Clara

Written by Evelyn Rothstein

Illustrated by Elizabeth Uhlig

> **About the book**: Clara grew up around the time of World War I, in a poor Jewish community in Russia. Family life was filled with hardships. Clara wanted to go to school, wear fashionable clothes and live a better life. And although there were many obstacles to this dream — the loss of her mother, soldiers who occupy the family's home, and a very difficult trip across Europe-- Clara and her younger sister eventually made the long journey to America.
>
> Published by Marble House Editions, paperback, July 2009, For ages 6-10

CHAPTER ONE: RESPONDING TO THE CULTURES OF THE TECHNOLOGICAL CLASSROOM

DAVE LEARNS SPANISH

About the book: Evelyn Rothstein's father, Dave, was an ambitious young man who lived on the Lower East Side. In this story, 18-year-old Dave is determined to get a good job by developing skills in Spanish and typing. But Spanish was only the first of many new languages for Dave. As an adult, he was to master twenty languages, and eventually became known as "Mr. Translator" in New York City's business world.

Published by Marble House Editions, paperback, July 2011, For ages 10 through 14.

Written by **Evelyn Rothstein**
Illustrated by **Elizabeth Uhlig**

Clara's Great War Published by Marble House Editions, paperback, , July 2011For ages 10 through 14.

About the book: *Clara's Great War* is the story of an eleven year-old girl and her family during World War I in Russia. In order to survive, Clara and her family must make room for enemy soldiers to use their home as a hospital. Clara, whose mother has died, is forced to play the role of cook, housekeeper, and helpmate to the doctor who is attending to wounded soldiers. During these times of scarce food and constant danger, Clara, who dreams of going to America, must wait out the war and not lose hope that her dream will come true.

Written by **Evelyn Rothstein**
Illustrated by **Elizabeth Uhlig**

FIGURE 1.11 FRAME FOR TELLING A CLASSMATE, FRIEND, OR FAMILY MEMBER ABOUT A BOOK WITH A CULTURAL THEME OR SETTING

I WOULD RECOMMEND....

(Title) _____ by (Author)_____

is one of the most (adjective or descriptor)_____ books for learning about _____.

The central character is _____ who _____.

In addition, there is _____ who _____.

The author has set this story in _____ during _____.

From the author's description of the time and setting, I learned (became aware, realized) _____.

For example, _____.

I urge you to read this book so that we can discuss many ideas, such as _____,

_____, and _____,

Culture and Spirituality

We are often guarded and sensitive about teaching spirituality or aspects of religion in our schools. Yet our schools revolve around days and holidays that have their basis in spiritual ideas and celebrations. However, many of our "diverse" cultures don't have their own special days mentioned and many teachers may not be knowledgeable about other people's celebrations or spiritual customs.

Once again, we recommend that to involve your students in this major aspect of humanity, you begin with a Taxonomy, preferably early in the school year, and have the students research and list the various celebrations held around the world. From the Taxonomy, students can do research, interview classmates and adults, collect artifacts, learn songs, and truly celebrate the world's celebrations. Figure 1.12 is a START-UP TAXONOMY. Ongoing research is necessary and your students will be captivated by this global search and journey. To help your students organize their research, we have added Figure 1.13, PROFILE OF A HOLIDAY, CELEBRATION, OR FESTIVAL.

Figure 1.12, START-UP TAXONOMY OF A SPIRITUAL CELEBRATION, FESTIVITY, OR HOLIDAY.

	SPIRITUAL CELEBRATION, FESTIVITY, OR HOLIDAY
A	
B	Boxing Day
C	Christmas, Children's Day
D	Diwali
E	Emancipation Day
F	
G	Good Friday
H	Hanukah
I	'Id at-Fatr
J	
K	Kwanzaa
L	
M	Magha Puja Day
N	Navajo Sing-Festival, Norooz
O	Odum Titun
P	Powamu Festival
Q	Ramadan, Rosh Hashana, Krishna Jayanti
R	
S	
T	Three Kings Day
U	
V	Vesak
W	
X	
Y	
Z	

FIGURE 1.13 PROFILE OF A HOLIDAY, CELEBRATION, OR FESTIVAL

Name of Holiday, Celebration, or Festival
_____

Major Group or Population Who Celebrates
_____

Places Where Predominantly Celebrated
_____

Reason(s) for Celebration
_____

Customs or Rituals of Celebration
_____

Brief History of
Celebration_____
Other Information

_____

Mapping Universals of Cultural

Access to the Internet and the plethora of media, networking, and information (*YouTube, Vimeo, Hulu, Pandora, Facebook, MySpace, blogs, Wikipedia* and so on) creates exciting opportunities for student projects on the universals of culture. Students can be given options to write about their own cultural heritages or search out new ones, basing their research on the "universals". To get started, you might want to have students do their first research project on those cultures, which, for various reasons, have been less integrated with other cultures. We suggest this starting point so that the students can realize that while we have "cultural differences," these differences are still part of the universals. As cultures mingle and integrate, they add to each other's knowledge, exchanging ideas, but still maintaining customs and ways that reveal their history and story. Figure 1.14 is a start-up TAXONOMY OF CULTURAL GROUPS which throughout their history or development have had clearly marked features of the universals of family, education, language, knowledge, celebrations, and spirituality. Add to this Taxonomy.

Figure 1.14 START-UP TAXONOMY OF WORLDWIDE CULTURAL GROUPS (Add more)

	WORLD-WIDE CULTURAL GROUPS
A	Amish, Aborigines
B	Bedouins, Bantu
C	
D	
E	
F	
G	
H	Hawaiian
I	Inuit, Ibo
J	
K	Kazakhs, Kurds
L	Lumbee
M	Mennonites, Maori, Masai
N	Navajo
O	Ojibway
P	Polynesian
Q	
R	
S	Sikhs, Samis, Sardinian, Samoan
T	Tongan, Tahitian
U	
V	
W	
X	
Y	
Z	Zulu

The **Cultural Group Profile** provides a framework for understanding the more profound cultural background to any content, and where it came from. Figure 1.4 (see *Writing As Learning* 2007)).

Figure 1.15 CULTURAL GROUP PROFILE

CULTURAL GROUP PROFILE
Name of Group _____
Original Habitat _____
Major Means of Livelihood_____
Type(s) of Dwellings _____
Language(s) _____
Form(s) of Governance _____
Major Roles and Tasks of Women _____
Major Roles and Tasks of Men _____
Significant Beliefs _____
Current Life Style _____
Types of Food _____
Major Festivals or Festivities _____
Members of Accomplishment _____
Other Information _____

The Family As Culture

When students enter our classroom they come from a family. All cultures live in some form of family organization. There are tribal families, clan families, extended families, nuclear families, single-parent families, and other groupings. One example of the unity among cultures is that families no matter what their make-up have multiple taxonomies for the members of their group. In English alone, the male parent can be: Father, Papa, Pappy, Poppy, Pa, Dad, Daddy and whatever other affectionate terms you might know or like. For the female parent, English has: Mother, Momma, Mommy, Mom, Mum, Mummy, Mammy, Ma, and whatever else you like. Naming the members of the family group is universal and when we help students recognize this universality they realize that they are culturally accepted and identified.

There are cultures and languages that have numerous words to express family relationships that other cultures and languages do not have and then there are languages that express these relationships in different ways. Figure 1.16 shows the similarities and differences between English and French words related to the family. Students can create their own types of family listings using background knowledge from their own family or through research.

CHAPTER ONE: RESPONDING TO THE CULTURES OF THE TECHNOLOGICAL CLASSROOM

Hello, Here are the members of

Bonjour, Ici sont les membres de

Figure 1.16 FAMILY MEMBERS IN ENGLISH AND FRENCH – What is similar? What is different?

MY FAMILY	MA FAMILLE
mom	maman
dad	papa
grandmother	grand-mère
grandfather	grand-père
great grandmother	arrière- grand-mère
great grandfather	arrière-grand-père
sister	soeur
brother	frère
cousin	cousin (male), cousine (female)
uncle	oncle
aunt	tante
sister-in-law	belle-soeur
brother-in-law	beau-frere
mother-in-law	belle-mère
father-in-law	beau-père

To further students' knowledge and understanding of family cultures, we have added information about diverse cultural groups that can serve as the basis for discussions on names, values, and beliefs, and will expose students to interesting differences as well as to the universals of all humanity. To get your students started, we have included information about family names in Hebrew (Figure 1.17), followed by family relationships among the Hopi Indians (Figure 1.18) and the people of Vietnam (Figure 1.19). Depending on where in the world you teach there are influxes of cultures perhaps different from the predominant ones and from which our students come from. These examples of Hebrew, Hopi and Vietnamese names should prompt you to work with your students to understand the culture of the families represented in your classroom. We have included the Hebrew writing of the names, which your students might find interesting and could serve as another project on different alphabets and writing systems.

Figure 1.17 FAMILY MEMBERS IN HEBREW

Hebrew is the language that is spoken in Israel and is also the language of the Hebrew Bible, sometimes known as The Old Testament. As in all languages, there are family member names. Most Hebrew-speaking families call their mother *eema* (אמא) and their father *abba* (אבא). A brother is *aḥ"*(אח), and a sister is *aḥot* (אחות). A son is called *ben* (בן) but can also be referred to more formally as *bar* (בר), which is where the term "bar mitzvah" comes from—meaning "son of good deeds." A daughter is bat (בת) as in "bat mitzvah or "daughter of good deeds".

The Hebrew word for grandmother is "savta" (סבתא), and the Hebrew word for grandfather is "sabba" (סבא). The Hebrew term for grandson is *neḥed* (נכד) and for granddaughter is *neḥda* (נכדה). An uncle is called dod (דוד), and an aunt is dodah (דודה). While uncles and aunts get their own titles, cousins are only seen as extensions of the uncles and aunts, and therefore are referred to more indirectly. A male cousin is referred to as *ben dod* (דוד בן), or the son of an uncle, and a female cousin is referred to as *bat dodah"*(דודה בת), or the daughter of an aunt

CHAPTER ONE: RESPONDING TO THE CULTURES OF THE TECHNOLOGICAL CLASSROOM

Figure 1.18 THE FAMILY RELATIONS ORDINANCE OF THE HOPI TRIBE

> It is the policy of the Hopi Tribe to demonstrate *respect*- "Kyap tsi" (Hopi) and "ag' ging" (Tewa), for members of the family and clan. The fundamental Hopi value of "kyap tsi" has long been practiced by the Hopi generations, and is reflected throughout Hopi tradition and culture. Abuse and violence against persons has a lasting and detrimental effect on (1) the individual who directly experiences the abuse, (2) the entire family and clan, who directly or indirectly experience the abuse, and (3) the Hopi Tribe, as the adverse effects of abuse and violence is perpetuated by succeeding generations and within Hopi society itself. The concept of "kyap tsi" and "ag' ging" incorporates a meaning of the family as sacred, or that which must be respected. The family, as a fundamental unit of Hopi society, is an inculcator of traditional values. Accordingly, the family must exist in harmony. It is in the Hopi Tribe's best interest to bring the family, the clan and the Hopi Tribe together, to help one another towards a healthy future and for the common good.

Figure 1.19 FAMILY RELATIONSHIPS IN VIETNAM

> Vietnamese people distinguish between the immediate family and the extended family. The Vietnamese immediate family includes not only the husband, wife, and their unmarried children, but also the husband's parents and the sons' wives and children, The extended family consists of the immediate family and close relatives who share the same family name and ancestors and who live in the same community.
>
> Vietnamese parents consider it a most important responsibility to train their children. By virtue of the principle of collective responsibility, the parents will bear the disgrace brought about by the activities of children who dishonor themselves just as they share the honor and fame of their virtuous and talented children.
>
> At an early age, children are taught by their parents to behave according to the principle of filial piety. The family is the school in which the child learns the respect rules in both behavior and linguistic response. Filial piety consists of loving, respecting, and obeying

one's parents. Talking back or acting contrary to the wishes of one's parents is evidence of lack of filial piety. The child who lacks filial piety is rejected and ostracized by other members of the family and community The worst insult which a Vietnamese can receive and by which he is deeply wounded is the expression "lack filial piety" (con bat hieu).

The notion of family ties is imprinted in the mind of the Vietnamese because of the importance of filial piety. Respect and love are demanded of young people to members of the parental generation and above. Uncles and aunts must be treated with respect as if they were one's own parents. In addition to the consciousness of blood relationships and the linguistic ties that reinforce kinship relationships and age seniority, members of the Vietnamese extended family are closely bound by the common veneration of the dead. Ancestor worship is a hyphen between the dead and the living and a strong tie between members sharing the same ancestry.

*Family relationships By Huynh Dinh Te **Source:**

http://www.geocities.com/SoHo/Den/5908/values/family.html (retrieved April, 2014)

Cultures Educate Their Children in the Ways and Mores of the Cultural Group

This concept can often be difficult to grasp, particularly when children of one culture enter the educational system of a different culture. Teachers and others can be puzzled (or intolerant) about what appears to be parents' "lack" of interest in their child's education or lack of knowledge about what the school expects. Often there can be a tension between the family's culture and the school culture, whether it's simply about food, time management, dress, holiday customs and demands, or just being "different."

But if we recognize that "cultural education" includes family wisdom (e.g. proverbs), games, songs, cooking, and the variety of customs in a household or geographic setting, we see learning. One of the great *unifiers* in a school is helping students develop a cognitive awareness of what they are learning at home and what their classmates are also learning in their homes. We'd like to start with a simple lesson in proverbs, because all cultures have their words of wisdom which are passed down through the generations and find their way into the culture's oral and written literature.

Proverbs From the Islamic World, Figure 1.20 is a collection of proverbs from predominantly Islamic cultures, which can be introduced as part of *Where in the World* (see Planning Wheel, page 27). You can introduce these proverbs to build knowledge of geography and awareness of cultural wisdom, and also help students develop interpretive skills of deep and inferential meanings. Available to you through the Internet are proverbs from around the world which students can search, interpret, and compare, an engaging and deep structure activity for building a variety of comprehension skills.

FIGURE 1.20 PROVERBS FROM THE ISLAMIC WORLD – A proverb is a short popular saying, usually of unknown and ancient origin, that expresses some truth or a useful thought. Read each proverb with a classmate and then each write your interpretation of what you think the proverb means. You also can check a world map and find the country where the proverb originated. Then do a search of proverbs from other parts of the world and share their meanings with classmates. www.creativeproverbs.com (retrieved November 10, 2014).

Proverb	Interpretation or Meaning
Saudi Arabia Write bad things that are done to you in the sand, but write the good things that happen to you on a piece of marble.	
Iran A blind person who sees is better than a seeing person who is blind.	
Lebanon If anyone is not willing to accept your point of view, try to see his or her point of view.	
Palestine Do good and throw it in the sea.	

Games Around the World – All children from all cultures learn games, first within their family setting, and later from whatever opportunities they have from the world around them. Games are socializing activities that often prepare the child, in many ways, for stepping into the world of school. As all of us have undoubtedly experienced, games bring us into the world of rules, give-and-take, accepting losing, and rejoicing over winning. Our learning of games is developmental, learned in the home and in our local surroundings. Games are the pre-cursors to counting, learning about our bodies, observing or learning gender differentiations, developing self-esteem or self-awareness, earning praise, and much more. And while games may seem an adjunct to school learning, they are an integral part of our cultural awareness. So, we say, "Let the Games Begin," both for fun and our intellectual stimulation inside the classroom as well as on the outside.

The educational connection to games is not hard to recognize. For expanding knowledge of word play, rhyming, rhythm, and poetry there are the jump rope and handclapping games generally associated with girls. Then there is the amazing and extensive vocabulary of the sports world—baseball, American football, soccer, basketball, hockey, and whatever else provides humans with fun and relaxation. There is the vast and multi-faceted world of games people play in the digital world, many of which are played in collaboration and/or competition with others from all over the world (i.e. World of Warcraft, Halo, Sims).

Even traditional games such as dominoes, chess, Yahtze, and numerous card games can all be played on-line with other people. Finally what can we say about the world of social gaming as found on Facebook. Farmville is played by millions of people who can only succeed in building their virtual farm where they share and enlist the assistance of others. To build a barn requires that friends send you the parts you need and they may come from your real neighbor across the street, your sibling in another state and a friend across the ocean. What matters is not how many games there are but how you can recognize opportunities to incorporate play into your classroom. Perhaps you're thinking, "I have a curriculum to follow" and "test preparation". We can't always be playing. Maybe not, but then we also know that "child play" is also the child's way of learning, so we suggest

CHAPTER ONE: RESPONDING TO THE CULTURES OF THE TECHNOLOGICAL CLASSROOM

both and have included several possibilities. Here is a listing from one of the many websites, followed by Figure 1.21, **CHANTS, CLAPPING GAMES, AND JUMP ROPE RHYMES,** with an example of each and a classroom activity for developing "school skills and learning" which we have named **AMERICAN GEOGRAPHY THROUGH SONGS** (Figure 1.22)

Figure 1.21 CHANTS, CLAPPING GAMES, AND JUMP ROPE RHYMES

CHANTS	CLAPPING GAMES	JUMP ROPE RHYMES
Walking Through Africa Walking through Africa, what do I see? I can see Inyoka looking at me. Walking through Africa, what do I see? I can see Ufudu looking at me. Walking through Africa, what do I see? I can see Indlovu looking at me. Walking through Africa, what do I see? I can see iIkhozi looking at me. (Zulu chant from South Africa)	**Hambone** Hambone, Hambone, have you heard? Papa's gonna buy me a mockingbird. If that mockingbird don't sing, Papa's gonna buy me a diamond ring. If that diamond ring don't shine, Papa's gonna buy me a fishing line. Hambone, Hambone, where you been? Around the world and I'm going again.	**Teddy Bear** Teddy Bear, Teddy Bear, turn around, Teddy Bear, Teddy Bear, touch the ground Teddy Bear, Teddy Bear, show your shoe Teddy Bear, Teddy Bear, that will do! Teddy Bear, Teddy Bear, go upstairs- Teddy Bear, Teddy Bear, say your prayers- Teddy Bear, Teddy Bear, turn out the lights- Teddy Bear, Teddy Bear, say good-night!

Figure 1.22 AMERICAN GEOGRAPHY THROUGH SONGS

With the help of the Internet, every classroom can learn lots of geography and have fun while learning. For example, go to this website and listen to Tim Pacific singing The 50 States and Capitals Song. You can check each capital's exact location and do a research project on a capital city that interests you. You can also research a song from your own state or city or river or mountain.

1. Montgomery, Alabama
2. Juneau, Alaska
3. Phoenix, Arizona
4. Little Rock, Arkansas
5. Sacramento, California
6. Denver, Colorado
7. Hartford, Connecticut
8. Dover, Delaware
9. Tallahassee, Florida
10. Atlanta, Georgia
11. Honolulu, Hawaii
12. Boise, Idaho
13. Springfield, Illinois
14. Indianapolis, Indiana
15. Des Moines, Iowa
16. Topeka, Kansas
17. Frankfort, Kentucky
18. Baton Rouge, Louisiana
19. Augusta, Maine
20. Annapolis, Maryland
21. Boston, Massachusetts
22. Lansing, Michigan
23. St. Paul, Minnesota
24. Jackson, Mississippi
25. Jefferson City, Missouri
26. Helena, Montana
27. Lincoln, Nebraska
28. Carson City, Nevada
29. Concord, New Hampshire
30. Trenton, New Jersey
31. Santa Fe, New Mexico
32. Albany, New York
33. Raleigh, North Carolina
34. Bismarck, North Dakota
35. Columbus, Ohio
36. Oklahoma City, Oklahoma
37. Salem, Oregon
38. Harrisburg, Pennsylvania
39. Providence, Rhode Island
40. Columbia, South Carolina
41. Pierre, South Dakota
42. Nashville, Tennessee
43. Austin, Texas
44. Salt Lake City, Utah
45. Montpelier, Vermont
46. Richmond, Virginia
47. Olympia, Washington
48. Charleston, West Virginia
49. Madison, Wisconsin
50. Cheyenne, Wyoming

CHAPTER 2

EPOCHS OF CHANGE AND EDUCATIONAL IMPLICATIONS

Great epochs of change have taken place over thousands of years, marching slowly across history. But now the electronic changes of the past 100 years have been equal to the thousands of years before. All of these epochs of change would obviously change the focus and needs of educating our children. A powerful significance of these epochs, however, has been its unequal distribution across cultures and the effect of this inequality on the wealth and well-being of different populations. Jared Diamond, in *Guns, Germs, and Steel* (1999) provides an in-depth history and understanding of these epochal changes and the effects on our lives today and has influenced us to focus on the inventions of the past that have been a significant force in shaping the educational needs of humans worldwide.

- The wheel for greater distance transportation
- Agriculture for changing societies from hunters/gatherers to allow for permanence of location
- Alphabets and iconic symbols to keep records of events and goods and eventually share ideas
- Weaponry and its effect on technology
- Inventions such as electricity to connect us to others and microscopes, and telescopes to change our views of the small world and the larger universe
- Horseless locomotion (cars, airplanes, rockets) to move us with great speed
- Electronics, particularly the micro-processor which has allowed the advent of personal computing and the development of a Digital Age and global communication

We expand on these ideas below which you can share with your students as appropriate to their age and what you are teaching. Included are activities to get you started.

The Wheel and the Advance of Transportation

The invention of the wheel changed the history of humankind, allowing those populations that also had access to horses, an advantage over other populations (Diamond, 1999). By having a horse and wheels, people could navigate over larger distances, intermingle with other populations, and, of course, conquer the "weaker" populations. New "technology" arose—wagons, chariots, coaches—bringing about occupations of wheelwrights, saddle makers, riders, blacksmiths, among others, and bringing about a new "education" for its population.

THE WHEEL

Based on diagrams on ancient clay tablets, the earliest known use of this essential invention was a potter's wheel that was used at Ur in Mesopotamia (part of modern day Iraq) as early as 3500 BC. The first use of the wheel for transportation was probably on Mesopotamian chariots in 3200 BC. It is interesting to note that wheels may have had industrial or manufacturing applications before they were used on vehicles.

A wheel with spokes first appeared on Egyptian chariots around 2000 BC, and wheels seem to have developed in Europe by 1400 BC without any influence from the Middle East. Because the idea of the wheel appears so simple, it's easy to assume that the wheel would have simply "happened" in every culture when it reached a particular level of sophistication. However, this is not the case. The great Inca, Aztec and Maya civilizations reached an extremely high level of development, yet they never used the wheel. In fact, there is no evidence that the use of the wheel existed among native people anywhere in the Western Hemisphere until well after contact with Europeans.

> Since the invention of the wheel over 5000 years ago, it's been impossible to imagine the world without it — that includes the sporting world! From BMX bikes to Formula One racing, wheels offer an exciting dimension to sports. There are great deals of sports that require equipment with wheels — where would Grand Prix be without the motorcycle? Or the Tour de France without the bicycle? In fact, sports on wheels have become so sophisticated that we can now enjoying watching wheelchair tennis players glide across courts with ease and grace.
>
> http://www.ideafinder.com/history/inventions/wheel.htm (retrieved November 20, 2013)

Figure 2.1—The Wheel in Our Lives is a triple Taxonomy, which your students can use as part of a Metacognition Frame to write about what they know about a wheeled vehicle. The **Metacognition Frame, Figure 2.2.** follows the Taxonomy, followed by **Figure 3, Reasons, Causes, Results.**

Figure 2.1 – WHEELS AND VEHICLES IN OUR LIVES –

Instructions to Students – Complete this Taxonomy by adding an occupation or hobby and a sport or sports that are associated with the vehicle's use. Use the Metacognition Frame that follows to write a statement about what you know about a particular vehicle. You can also do further research for a full project on different wheels and vehicles. There are two examples to help you get started. You can also add to this Taxonomy.

	VEHICLES AND WHEELS	OCCUPATIONS, HOBBIES, USERS	SPORTS (if any)
A	automobile, airplane	mechanic, designer	car racing
B	bicycle, buggy, baby buggy	bicyclist driver baby	bicycle racing, BMX buggy races
C	coach, chariot, cart		
D			
E			
F	ferris wheel		
G	go-cart		
H	helicopter humvee		
I			
J	jitney		
K			
L			
M	motorcycle		
N			
O			
P	paddlewheel boat pushcart perambulator		
Q			
R	roller blades		
S	skateboard, surrey stroller		
T	tractor, tank, train, truck tricycle		
U			
V			
W	wagon		
X			
Y			
Z			

Figure 2.2. Metacognition Frame of a Wheeled Vehicle

I know that I know something about a (pick your own vehicle)_____.

First I know that it has the following parts: _____.

I also know that it was invented or made during (time period(s)_____.

In order to drive or operate this vehicle, a person has to _____.

This vehicle is used mainly to _____.

Now you know _____.

(Find an illustration of your vehicle on the Internet or any other source you may have)

A valuable strategy from the Planning Wheel is *Reasons, Causes, Results*, and a simple essay format that allows students to explain the significance of events, changes, or inventions of a particular epoch. Figure 2.3 is a model of a FRAME for writing about the importance of the wheel in human development and learning.

FIGURE 2. 3 - The Significance of the Wheel in Expanding Human Knowledge.

Use this Frame to tell about significance of the wheel.

> Since the invention of the wheel over 5000 years ago, it's been impossible to imagine the world without it. I (We) can cite three reasons why the invention of the wheel expanded human knowledge.
>
> First, once an animal (e.g. horse, ox, llama) could be hooked up to a wheeled vehicle, By having a (horse and wagon, a person would be able to learn_____.
>
> In addition, an animal-drawn wheeled vehicle could gradually be improved by _____ and people would now know more about_____
>
> Finally, the wheel would be part of vehicles that would not need animals, such as _____. With these wheeled vehicles, humans would learn/know/realize_____.
>
> From these reasons, we can conclude (better understand, predict)_____.

Agriculture - From Hunting and Gathering to Permanent Settlements

From the early descent of humans till about 11,000 years ago, hunting wild animals and gathering wild plants was the only means of having food. Not till about 11,000 years ago, were there humans who planted for consumption and used domesticated animals to help with production of food (1999, Diamond). This enormous change in the ability to grow and harvest food and raise and use domestic animals would bring about vast economic and cultural changes, including the widespread reduction of hunting and gathering. Agriculture brought about concepts of land ownership resulting in differences in wealth as well as in aggression. The development of agriculture was dependent on climate and the already availability of annual plants (1999, Diamond). The area known today as the Fertile Crescent in the Eurasian section around the western Mediterranean had the advantage of climate and significant botanical wealth of seed-bearing grasses.

Furthermore, this gift of plant life and climate was also accompanied by "domesticable" animals. Domestication of animals (sheep, cows, horses) would have major consequences for human history—namely that big wild animal species such as zebras and peccaries have never been domesticated and that the successful domesticates were almost exclusively Eurasian (157, 1999, Diamond). And although there were other areas with advantageous climates for plants (California, Australia, Chile), the absence of animals for domestication limited major agriculture in comparison to the Eurasian lands.

Culturally, in many agricultural groups, role differences between men and women sharpened, with women often the "workers" of the land and men still remaining the hunters. However, with hunting gradually diminishing, men often were able to pursue other activities, one of which would eventually be time for "study", at least among those populations where the labor-intensive aspects of agriculture could be left to the women. Centers of learning followed and would increase as writing systems developed and grew, which we discuss later in this chapter.

Since agriculture and domestic animals continue to play an enormous role in every human's life today, we believe that all students, of all ages, can be engaged in learning about these two aspects of our lives and its cultural impact. Learning about plants and animals can be integrated into all aspects from the curriculum including science, social studies, nutrition, mathematics, and *culture*. We previously suggested a Taxonomy on foods (Figure 1.2) and we continue here with additional strategies related to plants and animals and their roles in everyone's life.

Students in the early grades in particular (but not limited to them) are always interested in animals, especially "farm animals" that they might have seen or they might even "own" in their families. Domestic animals are in English nursery rhymes (e.g. Old MacDonald), and the vocabulary of these animals often provide male, female, and "baby" names. Young children frequently have stuffed animals that they treasure and "live" with. So in Figure 2.4 we start with a Taxonomy of Domesticated Animals with their gender names (when available) and their names when they are "young." In Figure 2.5 we give a sample Defining Format to help students describe the characteristics of one of these domestic animals and in Figure 2.6 we have set up a five-column Taxonomy of domesticated animals in English, Spanish, Italian, and French, with the blank column for naming these animals in any other language or languages. After these Taxonomies, we have added a "Where in the World" activity for learning about the "grasses" that provide us with food (Figure 2.7). We think your students will have fun while learning these ideas and becoming immersed in culture-related information.

Figure 2.4 – DOMESTICATED ANIMALS Instructions to Students - Here are the names of animals that have been "domesticated" to live on a farm or help humans do their work or chores. Find the male, female and "baby" names if they exist. Use the Internet to help you. There are two examples to get you started. You can add other domesticated animals if you find them on the Internet or other source.

MOST COMMON NAMES	MALE NAME	FEMALE NAME	"BABY" NAME
cow	bull or steer	cow	calf
chicken			
camel			
duck			
donkey			
elephant			
goat			
goose			
horse			
hog			
llama			
mule			
ox			
pig	boar	sow	piglet
reindeer			
sheep			
turkey			

FIGURE 2.5. DEFINING FORMAT-- WHAT IS A LLAMA?

Here is a Defining Format to define a llama to a "Martian", someone who has never seen one. Use this model to define another animal from the Taxonomy (Figure 2.4) to your own "Martian." The Internet can be a source for your information. You will probably have to read an article from the Internet slowly and carefully and then select what you think is the most important information to select for the "Martian."

QUESTION	CATEGORY	CHARACTERISTICS
What is a llama? A llama is an	animal that	1) is a four-legged mammal 2) is related to the Bactrian and Dromedary camels of Asia 3) comes in different colors such as brown, red, black, or white 4) lives mainly in Peru 5) has been domesticated by the Inca Indians for transportation and carrying goods 6) has been brought to the United States for use as pack animals in the mountains 7) provides wool for humans 8) can be used to guard sheep 9) (add more if you wish)

FIGURE 2.6. TAXONOMY OF THE NAMES OF DOMESTICATED ANIMALS IN FIVE LANGUAGES - You might like to know the names of some of the domesticated animals in different languages. Here is a start-up list in English, Spanish, Italian, French, and German. There is also a column for you to add the names of these animals in another language as part of your research. Have fun expanding your linguistic knowledge.

ENGLISH	SPANISH	ITALIAN	FRENCH	GERMAN*	YOUR CHOICE
chicken	pollo	pollo	poulet	Huhn	
cow	vaca	mucca	vache	Kuh	
duck	pato	anatra	canard	Ente	
goat	cabrio	capra	chevre	Ziege	
horse	caballo	cavallo	cheval	Pferd	
pig	cerdo	maiale	couchon	Schwein	
sheep	oveja	pecora	mouton	Schaf	
Add one more					

*German nouns are written with a capital letter

GRASSES (a.k.a. cereals or grains) THAT GIVE US FOOD

You may think that only animals eat grass, but humans do too, except that these "grasses" are the kinds that we usually think of as products that we use for bread or cereals such as oats, wheat, rye, couscous, and many others. Grains are mostly grasses cultivated for their edible grains or seeds. Cereal grains are grown in greater quantities and provide more energy worldwide than any other type of crop. They are therefore staple crops, providing a rich source of carbohydrate. In some developing nations, grain constitutes practically the entire diet of poor people in contrast to developed nations, where cereal consumption is more moderate but still substantial.

Humans in almost all parts of the world have learned to *cultivate* these grasses to provide food for themselves and also to *export* to other people. Figure 2.7 is a map that shows where wheat and rice--the most common grasses or grains-- are grown. Figure 2.8 is a Taxonomy of the main cultivated grasses or grains. Select one of the grasses from the Taxonomy and have the student complete the Defining Format (Figure 2.9) with as much information as the can find. Have the students find a recipe for one of the grains to use at home or share. Figure 2.10 shows an example of how to make a tortilla, a recipe made with the grain of maize, also called corn. Share the recipes and, if possible, bring a taste of these foods to the class.

Figure 2.7 REGIONS OF THE WORLD WHERE WHEAT AND RICE ARE GROWN

This map shows wheat production throughout the world. The map shows that wheat is more adapted to different environmental conditions and can grow over much larger areas of the world compared to rice. So, even though it grows best when it is warm with plenty of light and water, wheat can be grown successfully under less favorable conditions.

Figure 2.8. TAXONOMY OF GRAINS FOR HUMAN CONSUMPTION

	GRAINS OF THE WORLD
A	maranth
B	barley, buckwheat
C	couscous
D	durum
E	einkorn
F	
G	
H	
I	
J	
K	
L	
M	millet, maize
N	
O	oats
P	
Q	quinoa
R	rice
S	sorghum, spelt
T	teff
U	
V	
W	wheat
X	
Y	

The word *cereal* comes from Ceres, the Roman goddess of agriculture and harvest.

Figure 2.9 DEFINING FORMAT FOR TELLING ABOUT A SPECIFIC GRAIN

Use this model to write your own Defining Format for a different grain.

QUESTION	CATEGORY	CHARACTERISTICS
What is sorghum? Sorghum is a	species or type of grain that	1) is one of the five top cereal grains in the world 2) originated in Africa, mainly in Egypt 3) is now grown in Asian and the Americas 4) is a tall plant over six feet tall 5) has also been bred as a dwarf plant 6) add more if you wish

Figure 2.10 RECIPES FOR MAKING TORTILLAS

Here's a recipe that's very popular in Mexico. You may try to make this at home with your family. You can also bring in a favorite recipe to your class and exchange it for a recipe from one of your classmates.

Before You Start

You will need a special corn flour called masa harina, which you can buy at Mexican markets and is specially made for tortillas. You can make the tortillas by hand, but making them will be easier if you have a tortilla press, which you can also get in a Mexican market. If you don't have a press, you can roll out the masa (or dough) with a rolling pin between pieces of wax paper.

Ingredients:
2 Cups **Masa Flour**
¼ Teaspoon **Baking Soda**
1 ½ Cups **Warm Water**

Tools: Wax Paper, Large Skillet, Spatula, Bowl and Dishtowel
(Serving Size: 16 to 18 tortillas)

1. Put 2 cups of masa flour in a large bowl.
2. Mix in a ¼ teaspoon of baking soda.
3. Add about 1-½ cups of very warm water to the flour.
4. Mix in the water and let it sit for five minutes.

Knead the dough by pressing it with your fingers and the palm of your hands.
Add a little water if the dough gets dry.
Take a small piece of dough, about the size of a plum and shape it into a ball.
Continue till you have about 16 to 18 balls.

Heat a griddle or large skillet
Hold the tortilla in your hand. Remove the wax paper on each side.
Slide the tortilla into the skillet.

Cook the tortilla for 30 seconds.
Flip with a spatula and cook for another 30 seconds.
Remove the tortilla to a dishtowel.
Fill the tortillas with some meat or vegetables and fold in half.

Re-warm your tortilla in the skillet and eat immediately. Enjoy.

Alphabets and Icons for Keeping Records and Sharing Ideas

In the long of history of human development and inventions, nothing would impact as much on human life as the creation of writing systems. Writing systems would keep a record of what we have, what we have done and are doing, and what we believe. Writing would allow us, for the first time, to transcend the spoken, to know about other people, other places, and gather other ideas and values. As succinctly stated by Diamond, "writing brings power to [a] society by making it possible to transmit knowledge with far greater accuracy and detail, from more distant lands and more remote times" (1999, 215).

Writing would also change the lives of children because, until the invention of writing, children could learn everything they needed to know at home or in the fields, or as we have joked, "in summer camp." But as writing developed, the home and fields did not suffice for children learning the complexities of print. Only schools could impart the information and concentrated instruction that was required to "read" the abstract symbols that heretofore only *scholars* had mastered.

The Major Writing Systems

There are three major writing systems known as alphabetic, iconic or logographic, and syllabary. The most common system today is alphabetic which uses symbols to represent phonemes (sounds), but may also include icons such as $. %, +, @, among others. An icon is a symbol that represents a whole word as in Chinese and Japanese, and was the major part of the system called hieroglyphics. Syllabaries use symbols to represent syllables, most common of which today is the Japanese Kana Syllabary. Braille is mainly an alphabetic system for blind people using raised dots in different arrangements to represent letters. And sign language has been developed by people with hearing impairments.

The first writing systems did not have a proper alphabet, but were rather similar to Asian languages such as Chinese, where each symbol represents a word rather than a letter. These alphabets date back to 3500 BC, when the Sumerians and the Egyptians came up with a system of writings that included hieroglyphs and wedge-shaped symbols. The first alphabet was invented by the Phoenicians around 1000 BCE. This alphabet is considered the origin of the Greek and Latin alphabets, as we know it, although there were some notable differences. The Phoenician alphabet had 22 letters and only consonants to represent the consonant phonemes of the Phoenician language.

Making students aware of writing systems can expand students' cultural and linguistic knowledge. Learning an alphabet other than the one derived from Latin (as used in English) is not merely challenging, but leads to greater understanding of one's own alphabet and to the historic forces or events that brought about different alphabets. And since alphabetic systems are likely to include icons, having students learn several Chinese and Japanese icons, or others, opens up opportunities for high-level discussions about the reasons for these different types of symbolic representations. In addition, these discussions can also be a springboard to understanding the origins of and purposes for the many mathematical symbols, many of which your students will encounter. To get you and your students engaged in exploring different writing systems (which are now available on the Internet) we have set out three alphabets that are interrelated by history.

The Greek Alphabet

The Greek alphabet emerged around 1200 BCE and during the time of the epics of Homer, (800 BCE). It was an adaptation of the Phoenician alphabet to which the Greeks introduced vowel letters to make the language readable in Greek. Figure 2.11 shows the letters of the ancient Greek alphabet, most of which are still in use today in modern Greek. Intermediate and older students will enjoy learning this alphabet, which still has popularity in fraternities. A fun activity is to have the students try to write their names in the upper case Greek letters and figure out the phonemic system.

FIGURE 2.11 Letters of the Greek Alphabet How many of these letters do you recognize?

THE GREEK ALPHABET

Αα	Alpha	**Νν**	Nu
Ββ	Beta	**Ξξ**	Xi
Γγ	Gamma	**Οο**	Omicron
Δδ	Delta	**Ππ**	Pi
Εε	Epsilon	**Ρρ**	Rho
Ζζ	Zeta	**Σσς**	Sigma
Ηη	Eta	**Ττ**	Tau
Θθ	Theta	**Υυ**	Upsilon
Ιι	Iota	**Φφ**	Phi
Κκ	Kappa	**Χχ**	Chi
Λλ	Lambda	**Ψψ**	Psi
Μμ	Mu	**Ωω**	Omega

Can you read these names?

ΡΑΦΑΕΛ   ΣΑΜΑΝΘΑ

The Latin alphabet is used by the Romance languages of Spanish, Portuguese, Italian, French, Rumanian, and related languages such as Catalan and Provencal. In addition, there are the Germanic languages, which include German, English, Dutch, Flemish, Danish, Norwegian, and Swedish, and related languages such as Frisian. Through the forces of history (which you and your students can check out), Estonian, Finnish, Turkish, Hungarian, Croatian, Polish, Latvian, and Lithuanian also use the Latin alphabet.

The Latin alphabet began with the Etruscans, in the Roman Republic times, around the 5th century BCE. As the Roman Empire extended throughout Europe, so did the Latin alphabet, eventually reaching all the way to Romania and England. Throughout the following centuries, changes were made to the Latin alphabet, until it eventually reached the form it has today, with modifications made by different languages such as accent marks and doubling of letters.

Originally the Latin alphabet consisted of the following 21 letters:

A B C D E F Z H I K L M N O P Q R S T V X

About 250 BCE the letter Z was dropped because in the Latin of this period there was not a specific phoneme that would require its usage. On the other hand, a new letter, G, made by adding a bar to the lower end of C, was placed in the position of Z. After the 1st century BC, when the Greek-speaking world was incorporated into the Roman Empire, a large number of Greek words penetrated the Latin language. The symbols Y and Z were introduced from the Greek alphabet and were placed at the end of the alphabet. Thus, at the beginning of the Christian era the Latin script had 23 letters:

A B C D E F G H I K L M N O P Q R S T V X Y Z

Three new letters were permanently added to the English alphabet during the Middle Ages. -- J,U, and W-- as new phonemes and words came into the English language. . W was invented by Norman scribes to represent the Anglo-Saxon phoneme [w] and to differentiate it from the [v] sound. At the end of the 15th century. the English alphabet was finally fixed as consisting of 26 letters:

A B C D E F G H I J K L M N O P Q R S T U V W X Y Z

Cursive writing and lower case letters did not exist until the Middle Ages, and many letters did double duty, standing for more than one phoneme. The Latin alphabet has remained constant since then. The Internet is a powerful source of alphabet information, which students can find very engaging and we suggest that students make use of the multiple sources for art and research projects. In addition, the availability of fonts on the computer can be used creatively and uniquely (see Figure 2.12 depicting different fonts).

Cursive script developed early in the Middle Ages and was constantly modified to permit greater speed. The changes of Latin writing in the course of the centuries was influenced by the nature of the tool also, primarily the pen, and the material of writing was mainly papyrus and parchment from the 14th century onward. It was the pen, with its preference for curves that eliminated the angular forms; it was the papyrus, and still more the parchment or vellum, and, in modern times, paper, that made these curves possible.

> Amy Burton **Camilla** Dominique *Esran* Florence Gerald **Harvey**
> Isabella Juan Katrina **Luisa** Mai-lan Norman *Omar* Pietr Quintana
> Raoul Sherry **Tawonda** Ulysses **Verena** Willy Xena *Yu Tang*
> Zorina

The population that speaks Slavic languages is divided into two alphabetic groups, based on whether they are predominantly Roman Catholic or Greek or Russian Orthodox, so that Croatians and Poles use the Latin letters, whereas Russians, Ukrainians, Bulgarians, and Serbians use the Cyrillic alphabet which consists of letters from the Latin and Greek, plus letters designed specifically for the phonemes of these languages. The Cyrillic

CHAPTER TWO EPOCHS OF CHANGE AND EDUCATIONAL IMPLICATIONS

alphabet is also used for two non-Slavic languages, Kazakh and Mongolian, because of the influence of Russia.

In Russia, Cyrillic was first written in the early Middle Ages in clear-cut, large legible letters. Later a succession of cursive forms developed. In the early eighteenth century, under Peter the Great, the forms of letters were simplified and regularized, with some appropriate only to Greek being removed. Further unnecessary letters were expunged in 1918, leaving the alphabet as it is today—still in use in Slavic Orthodox countries.

Figure 2.13 illustrates the letters of the Cyrillic alphabet, which only have one case, with the exception of two letters. A challenging, but fun activity is to have the students write their names in Greek and Cyrillic and then discuss what "spelling" problems they had and how they solved these problems. Try it!

Figure 2.13 LETTERS OF THE CYRILLIC (RUSSIAN) ALPHABET- Make a chart, if you wish, of letters that are the same in all three alphabets and letters that are different. If you really feel challenged, make a chart of Greek and Cyrillic letters that are the same.

А а (A)	Р р (R)
Б б (B)	С с (S)
В в (V)	Т т (T)
Г г (G)	У у (U)
Д д (D)	Ф ф (F)
Е е (E)	Х х (KH)
Ё ё (YO)	Ц ц (TS)
Ж ж (ZH)	Ч ч (CH)
З з (Z)	Ш ш (SH)
И и (I)	Щ щ (SHCH)
Й й (Y)	ъ (-)
К к (K)	ы (Y)
Л л (L)	ь (')
М м (M)	Э э (E)
Н н (N)	Ю ю (YU or IU)
О о (O)	Я я (YA or IA)
П п (P)	

Alphabets of the Two Major Semitic Languages – Hebrew and Arabic

The Hebrew Alphabet

Hebrew and Arabic are cognate languages known also as Semitic languages, both with origins in the Middle East. The written Hebrew language goes back to early Biblical times. It diminished as a spoken language as a result of the destruction of the Second Temple in 79 C.E., but it continued as a written language with a vast literature for hundreds of years after. For over 2000 years, Hebrew was used by Jews mainly for prayers and scholarly readings and occasionally used by Jews from different parts of the world as a "Lingua Franca" or common language mainly for the purpose of trade.

The revival of Hebrew as a spoken language came about with a Jewish national movement when many European Jews immigrated to what was Palestine under Turkish rule in the 1880's. Ben-Yehuda, a revolutionary in Tsarist Russia, immigrated to Palestine in 1881 and set his goal to make Hebrew the spoken, as well as the written language of what would later become Israel. Today Modern Hebrew is written with the same script that was used in the Hebrew Bible for 2000 years and it also has cursive letters for handwriting. The Hebrew alphabet is also used for writing Yiddish, a German-based language spoken and was written by millions of Jews from the period of the Middle Ages until the Holocaust and continues to be spoken by small numbers of Jews in different parts of the world.

Figure 2.14 shows the letters of the Hebrew Alphabet. Hebrew is written right to left; it has no vowels, but pronunciation aids are often added. Hebrew letters have numerical vowels. The Hebrew alphabet is often called the "*alefbet*" because of its first two letters.

FIGURE 2.14 THE LETTERS OF THE HEBREW ALPHABET

The "Kh" and the "Ch" are pronounced as in German or Scottish, a throat clearing noise, not as the "ch" in "chair."

Note that there are two versions of some letters. Kaf, Mem, Nun, Pei and Tzadei all are written differently when they appear at the end of a word than when they appear in the beginning or middle of the word. The version used at the end of a word is referred to as Final Kaf, Final Mem, etc. The version of the letter on the left is the final version. In all cases except Final Mem, the final version has a long tail.

Like most early Semitic alphabetic writing systems, the alefbet has no vowels. People who are fluent in the language do not need vowels to read Hebrew, and most words written in Hebrew in Israel are written without vowels.

However, as Hebrew literacy declined, particularly after the Romans expelled the Jews from Israel, the rabbis recognized the need for aids to pronunciation, so they developed a system of dots and dashes called nikkud (points). These dots and dashes are written above, below or inside the letter, in ways that do not alter the spacing of the line. Text containing these markings is referred to as "pointed" text.

The Arabic Alphabet

The **Arabic alphabet** (Arabic: أبجدية عربية) is the script used for writing several languages of Asia and Africa and after the Latin alphabet, it is the second-most widely used alphabet around the world.

The alphabet was first used to write texts in Arabic, most notably the Koran, the holy book of Islam. With the spread of Islam, it came to be used to write many languages of many language families. (See sidebar). Although the Arabic alphabet as we know it today appears highly distinctive, it is actually related to the Latin, Greek, Phoenician, Aramaic, and Hebrew alphabets. Other languages – such as Farsi (Persian), Urdu and Malay – use adaptations of the Arabic script. The numerals used in most parts of the world – 1, 2, 3, etc – were originally Arabic, though many Arab countries today use Hindi numerals.

The Arabic script is written from right to left, in a cursive style, and includes 28 basic letters. Just as different handwriting styles and typefaces exist in the roman alphabet, the Arabic script has a number of different styles of calligraphy, including Naskh خط النسخ, Ruq'ah خط الرقعة, Thuluth خط الثُلث, Kufic الخط الكوفي, among others. Unlike cursive writing based on the Latin alphabet, the standard Arabic style is to have a substantially different shape depending on whether it will be connecting with a preceding and/or a succeeding letter, Figure 2.15 shows the modern Arabic alphabet.

SEVERAL OF THE LANGUAGES OTHER THAN ARABIC THAT USE THE ARABIC ALPHABET

Arwi (Sri Lanka)

Azerbajani (Iran)

Baloch (Malay)

FIGURE 2.15 THE ARABIC ALPHABET - The Arabic alphabet is read from right to left, top to bottom. Letters whose names appear highlighted in white are those which can't be joined on the left side. Letters with highlighted names in black change shape according to position in the word. Below this alphabet is a sample of Arabic text, showing how the letters are joined.

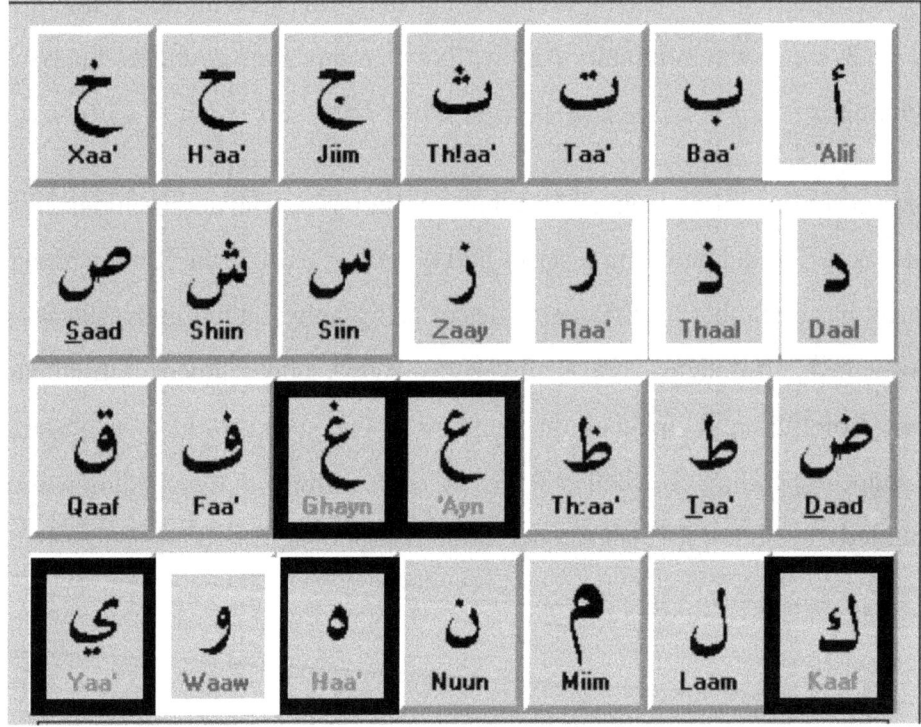

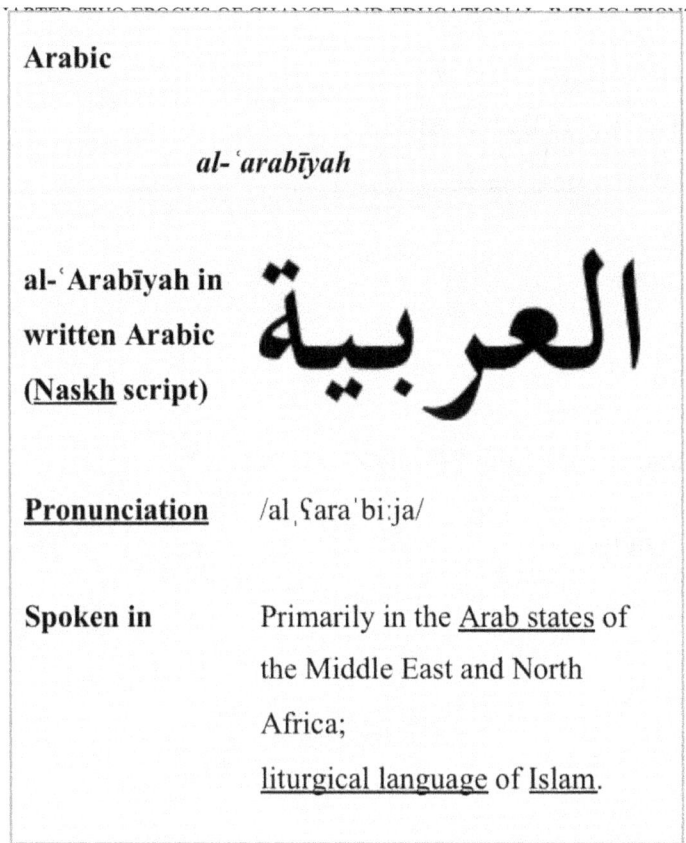

Having your students studying about languages and alphabets will enhance their global knowledge and enrich their understanding of the importance of literacy throughout the world. They will realize the diversity of languages and also recognize that every language is a complex system, but is always rule-governed and integral to the culture of the people who speak it. This knowledge helps them respect other cultures and understand that when ELL students come into our classrooms, they come with a language that they are proficient in. Figure 2.16 is a Language Profile for students to use as a first step in exploring a language they know little or nothing about. One copy of the Profile has been completed as a sample and a second copy is blank for you to copy.

FIGURE 2.16 LANGUAGE PROFILE FOR SWAHILI

Name of Language

Swahili

Countries or places where spoken

East Africa Coast, Uganda, Oman, United Arab Emirates

Number of people speaking the language

50 million

Family or branch

African Bantu with Arabic

Numbers from one to ten

One – moja   Two – mbili   Three – tatu   Four – nne   Five – tano   Six – sita

Seven – saba   Eight – nane   Nine – tisa   Ten – kumahg

Five other words and their English meaning

efere jambo [JAH-mbo] hello

kwaheri [kwah-HAY-ree] goodbye

simba [sim-bah] lion

shule SHOO-kay] school

rafiki [ra-FI-ki]

The word Swahili means coast and this language evolved along the east coast of Africa. The Disney movie *The Lion King* used the Swahili words Simba for the name of the lion and Rafiki for Simba's friend.

PROFILE OF A LANGUAGE (BLANK)

Name of Language
Countries or places where spoken
Number of people speaking the language
Family or branch
Numbers from one to ten
Five other words and their English meaning
Other Information

NON-ALPHABETIC WRITING

The most non-alphabetic writings that we are likely to see in our own environment are Chinese and Japanese. These forms of writing are frequently based on syllables and are considered syllabaries or logograms. Those of us who use alphabets usually refer to non-alphabetic symbols as "characters." Learning new writing systems for most people is very difficult and our discussion here is mainly to provide a brief comparison of the differences between alphabetic and non-alphabet writing. Our purpose here is to make students aware of how different peoples perceived ways to write and that these ways became part of their culture. Fortunately today, the Internet can be a simplified research tool for getting into the subject. We offer a brief description of Chinese and Japanese writing, merely to get you and your students started.

Chinese Characters

Chinese characters each represent a single syllable, and in the vast majority of cases a single morpheme (word). Most characters can be decomposed into two simpler characters, a *radical* vaguely indicating the meaning plus a *phonetic* symbol giving the approximate pronunciation.

Chinese 一 二 三 四 五 六 七 八 九 十
         yī èr sān sì wǔ liù qī bā jǐ shí

Although Chinese words may be formed by characters with basic meanings, a majority of words in Mandarin Chinese require two or more characters to write (thus are poly-syllabic) but have a meaning that is distinct from the characters they are made from. Chinese characters have also been used and in some cases continue to be used in other languages, most significantly Japanese (where a single character can represent several spoken syllables), and also, at times, in Korean, and Vietnamese.

Japanese Characters

The modern Japanese writing system uses three main scripts:

- Kanji, from Chinese characters,
- Hiragana, a set of symbols (syllabary) that approximates syllables which make up words
- Katakana, another syllabary used for foreign borrowings and other sounds.

To a small extent, modern written Japanese also uses the Latin alphabet—examples include abbreviations such as "CD" and "DVD".

Figure 2.17 shows an English sentence translated into Chinese and Japanese. Students will notice that there are both similarities and differences in the characters.

Figure 2.17 English, Chinese, Japanese

English

Today students all over the world are studying different languages. Chinese and Japanese students want to learn English. English-speaking students want to study Chinese and Japanese.

Chinese

世界各地的今天，学生学习不同的语言。汉语和日语学生想学习英语。英语为母语的学生要学习中国和日本。

Japanese

世界中で今日の学生のさまざまな言語を勉強している、中国語と日本語学生たちが英語を勉強したい、英語、学生を勉強したい話す中国語と日本語。

Syllabaries

Syllabaries developed as people realized that language can be written down just by recording the sounds. A relatively modern Syllabary was invented by Sequoyah, the Cherokee chief who wanted a writing system for his own people, allowing them to write in their native language. http://www.omniglot.com/writing/cherokee.htm (retrieved November 11, 2012). Figure 2.18 provides a brief history of the Cherokee Syllabary and its symbols.

Figure 2.18 The Cherokee Syllabary

This Syllabary was reputedly invented by George Guess, a.k.a. Chief Sequoyah, of the Cherokee, and was introduced in 1819. Sequoyah's descendants claim that he was the last surviving member of his tribe's scribe clan and the Cherokee Syllabary was invented by persons unknown at a much earlier date. By 1820 thousands of Cherokees had learned the Syllabary, and by 1830, 90% were literate in their own language. Books, religious texts, almanacs, and newspapers were all published using the syllabary, which was widely used for over 100 years.

Today the Syllabary is still used and efforts are being made to revive both the Cherokee language and the Cherokee Syllabary.

- Direction of writing: left to right in horizontal lines

- Used to write: Cherokee (Tsalagi Gawonihisdi), a Southern Iroquoian language spoken by around 22,500 people in North Carolina and Oklahoma.

Below this Syllabary are examples of other Syllabaries from different languages. There is an activity below you can do that is similar to Syllabary writing and is used today in text messaging.

Sanskrit	तृक	द	त्रि	चतुर्	पञ्च	षष्	सप्त	अष्ट	नव	दश
	éka	dvá	trí	catúr	páñca	ṣaṣ	saptá	aṣṭá	náva	dáça
Tibetan	གཅིག	གཉིས	གསུམ	བཞི	ལྔ	དྲུག	བདུན	བརྒྱད	དགུ	བཅུ
	gtšig	gñis	gsum	bži	lna	drug	bdun	brgyad	dgu	btšu
Thai	หนึ่ง	สอง	สาม	สี่	ห้า	หก	เจ็ด	แปด	เก้า	สิบ
	nyng²	sŏng³	sām³	si²	hâ⁴	hog²	ced²	pĕd²	kaž⁴	sib²
Burmese	တစ်	နှစ်	သုံး	လေး	ငါး	ခြောက်	ခုနစ်	ရှစ်	ကိုး	တစ်ဆယ်
	tiq	hniq	thoùn	lè	ngà	c'auq	k'un-hniq	shiq	kò	s'eh

TWO, FOUR, EIGHT, TEN

Here is a "shortcut" to writing English words that begin with the same syllables as the numbers 2, 4, 8, & 10. Use these words to write a letter to a friend or a make-believe story.

You can add your own words that use these number "syllables."

2	4	8	10
2day	4ce	b8	10der
2morrow	4ward	d8	10is
2n	4m	f8	10se
2t	4k	sl8	a10tion
2b	4th	cre8	de10tion
2l	4thright	negoti8	a10d

Louis Braille and Reading and Writing

For people with blindness or hearing losses, writing and reading were impossible until humans with these losses began to figure out how to help themselves and others who had similar losses. One of the great heroes for blind people was Louis Braille.

Louis Braille was born in France on January 4, 1809 and died January 6, 1852. He became blind at the age of 3, when he accidentally poked himself in the eye with a *stitching aw*l, one of his father's workshop tools. The injury wasn't thought to be serious until it got infected. Braille's other eye went blind because of what is known as *sympathetic ophthalmia.*

At age of 10, Braille earned a scholarship to the National Institute for the Blind in Paris, one of the first of its kind in the world. Here he learned basic craftsman skills and simple trades. He also learned how to read by feeling raised letters. However, the raised letters were made using paper pressed against copper wire so the students could never learn to write. And the letters weighed so much that a book might weight as much as a hundred pounds. The school had just 14 books, all of which Louis had read.

In 1821, Charles Barbier, a former Captain in the French Army, visited the school. Barbier shared his invention, called "night writing", which was a code of 12 raised dots and a number of dashes that let soldiers share top-secret information on the battlefield without having to speak. While the code was too difficult for Louis to understand, he developed his own idea of changing the number of raised dots to 6 to what we today we call Braille. The six-dot system allowed the reader to use a single fingertip to recognize all the dots making up a word. These dots consisted of patterns and made the system easy to learn, not only to read, but also to write.

Writing Braille

Braille may be produced using a *slate and stylus* in which each dot is created from the back of the page, writing in mirror image, by hand, or it may be produced on a Braille typewriter or *Perkins Brailler*, or produced by a Braille embosser attached to a computer..

The first ten letters of the alphabet and the digits 1 through 10 are formed using only the top four dots (1, 2, 4, and 5). Adding dot 3 forms the next ten letters, and adding dot 6 forms the last six letters (except w) and the words *and*, *for*, *of*, *the*, and *with*. Omitting dot 3 from the letters U-Z and the five word symbols form nine digraphs (ch, gh, sh, th, wh, ed, er, ou, and ow) and the letter w. Figure 2.19 illustrates the dot system of Braille. You can often find actual raised Braille on elevators and doorposts of buildings.

Figure 2.19 Letters in Braille

Braille has been adapted to write many different languages, including Chinese, and is also used for musical and mathematical notation. Its invention has also lead to new ways to help people with disabilities, such as detectable warnings, which are also known as 'Braille for the feet'.

Basic letters

a	b	c	d	e	f	g	h	i	j	k	l	m
n	o	p	q	r	s	t	u	v	w	x	y	z

Accented letters

à	â	ä/æ	è	é	ê	ë	ì	î
ï	ò	ô	ö/œ	ù	û	ü	ç	

Punctuation

,	;	:	.	!	()	? "	*	"	'	-	more	not

Numerals

1	2	3	4	5	6	7	8	9	0	and	for
										ow	bb

Special signs

letter sign	capital sign	numeral sign	numerical index sign	literal index	italic sign

Figure 2.20 The Manual Alphabet for People with Hearing Impairments

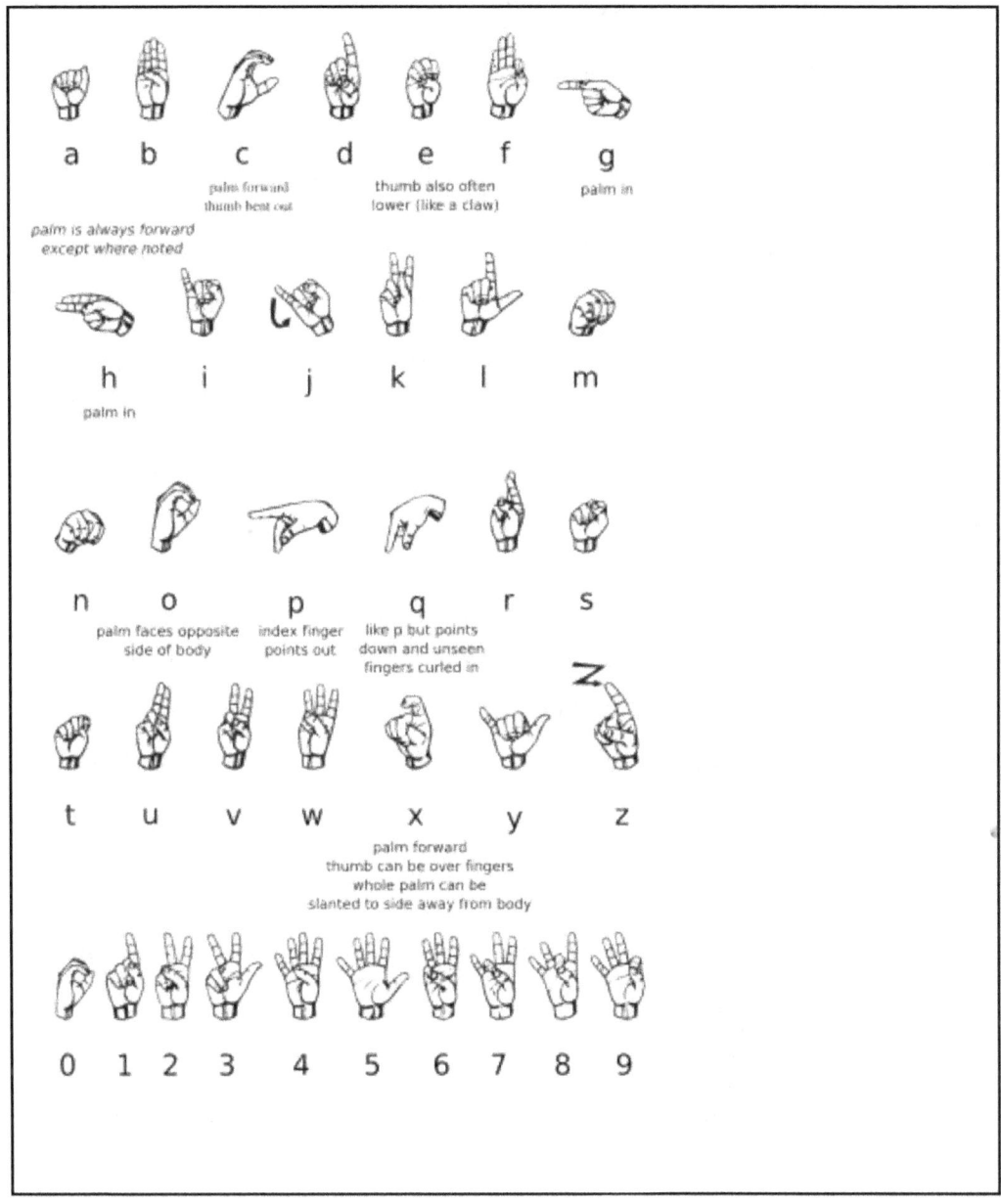

The Wheel and Writing—A Team in the Expansion of Education

The invention of the wheel, combined with the harnessing of animals such as the horse, mule, donkey, llama, camel, and reindeer. would provide the human with new mobility and greater exchange of knowledge among cultures. The ability to cultivate the land and establish "agriculture" as a livelihood offered humans a state of geographic permanence in contrast to hunting and gathering, eventually giving more people time for new pursuits.

One of the "new pursuits" resulted from the invention of writing. Writing systems would change the history and events of all humans, both uniting and disuniting cultures, and would bring about the concept of education and schools. Obviously, having writing would foster a meta-expansion of learning and knowledge, giving extraordinary advantages to those humans who were privileged to have access to this new form of communication. Sadly, for those who were denied—for reasons of poverty, gender, prejudice, bondage—writing became the wedge between the "haves and the have-nots."

We need to remember that while writing or literacy has contributed to the major aspects of schooling, it is having a language that requires us to have an formal *education*. Learning is a fundamentally human endeavor, but anyone living and working in a developed society must attain as much literacy as possible to open themselves to as much opportunity as possible.

Starting from shortly after infancy, children today have available to them a vast number of technology based toys and games that promote literacy. From *LeapPad* and the *Smartpen* to *Apple IPod Touch* and the *Nintendo DS* to name just a few (and the technology market for young children will only expand in the years to come), children as young as three years old can engage in learning letters, sounds, words and phrases of early literacy. By the time most children today have entered school, they will have had some interaction with some form of technology whether it be a cell phone or a house appliance, a smart pad, or a computer and who knows what else. The teenager in our classrooms has never lived without some of the technologies we marvel at and they are likely to come to us as literate users. In the author's practice, students today are using computer based essay scoring, interactive websites, blogs, virtual world interaction through gaming, and social networking to practice literacy and more specifically writing on often a daily basis. This is a wonderful opportunity to help students understand their own literacy and support their informal practice of writing connected to their day to day activity. The technology will continue to evolve and our job as educators is to grow with it. But along with the educational uses of technology are the advances in weaponry-- metaphorically a double-edged sword combining *knowledge and destruction.*

Weaponry –Technology and Its Effect on Technology

None of us can imagine a world without weaponry, a major tool that has insured warfare in at least some part of the world every day. Weaponry tools are in essence the human's earliest technology, and, as stated by Diamond (1999, 258) "technology begets more technology." Diamond expands on this concept by adding that

> "technology's history exemplifies what is termed an autocatalytic process: that is
>
> one that speeds up at a rate that increases with time, because the process catalyzes itself ."

He continues to further explain that the "main reason for autocatalysis is that new technologies and materials make it possible to generate still other technologies by recombination "(259). We may ask, of what importance is this statement to cultural responsiveness and the education of our children? Mainly, it is that all cultures have resorted to using or inventing some form of weaponry, either for defense or aggression, and the use of weapons has often been the determiner of what cultural group will dominate and control the lives and destinies of those who are the conquered or the dominated. In school, social studies is often the study of war, with the study of peace being secondary and transient.

So as part of looking at epochs of change and cultural issues, we suggest that students, already engaged in the world of digital technology, have the opportunity to view the history of weaponry and then enter into discussions of how to create possibilities for *social justice* along with the diminution of weapons and replacement with greater "communicative technologies" that have the potential of bringing us together. To start the overview and discussion, we present a chronology of ten weapons, where these weapons were initially developed, and a website for further information (Figure 2.21), followed by a research assignment for the students (Figure 2.22) Following Figure 2.21 are additional activities for your students.

FIGURE 2.21. CHRONOLOGY OF MAJOR WEAPONS OF WAR

340 BC -- Macedonians develop the catapult as a siege engine

904 -- The Chinese invent gunpowder

1327 – The cannon is developed in Europe

1733 – The first standardized pistol is used by the French military

1881 – The American inventor Hiram Maxim demonstrates the automatic machine gun

1916 – Professor Oskar Ursinus of Germany designs the fighter plane

1942 – General Walter Dornberger and German rocket scientist create the V-2 rocket

1945 – The atomic bomb is dropped on the Japanese city of Hiroshima

2007 – China develops the Land Attack Cruise Missile (LACM)

Figure 2.22 RESEARCH A WEAPON THAT HAS INCREASED THE DANGER OF WARFARE -- Research one of the weapons from Figure 2.21 (or any other weapon of interest to you) and use the Profile to place the information you have found. Then meet with a partner and exchange your findings and what you know about this weapon that you didn't know before.

Name of weapon _____

Year or years developed _____

Country or regions where developed _____

Group or people responsible for development _____

Description of weapon _____

Purpose or destructive power of weapon
_____

War(s) in which weapon was used
_____

Results of weapon's use
_____

Your own reaction to this weapon (You can start with "I believe that (name weapon) made warfare more dangerous in these three ways. Then discuss each way in as much detail as you can find or believe.)

Inventions – The Harnessing of Electricity and the Invention of the Microscope and Telescope

None of us in industrial societies can imagine a life without electricity. A day in which we are caught in an electrical blackout is the closest we can come to what life must have been like before the 19th century and only until late in that century--homes lit by candles and oil, warmth coming directly from fires, streets and landscapes lit only by the moon and stars, and, none of what today we call conveniences that we take for granted. And of course, before the microscope and telescope, few, if anyone, could imagine a world so small and so large. The harnessing of electricity and the inventions of the microscope and telescope would give new meaning to education and the expansion of knowledge. Studying the history of these developments and the changes they made in human life will give students opportunities to understand the global effects that resulted and will continue to result.

For activities we suggest:

- Myths about fire from different cultures
- Who's Who in the inventions and understanding of electricity
- Our electrical world today and its future
- Who's Who in the world of telescopes and microscopes
- "Microcosms" and "Macrocosms"

On the following page is a **A MYTH ADAPTED FROM THE KAROK AMERICAN INDIANS,,**Figure 2.23 followed by Figure 2.24, which uses Defining Format to answer the question "What is a myth?", followed by the question, "Why is the story How Coyote Stole Fire a myth? Figure 2.25 provides the student with a Frame for writing an original myth based on a specific "why" or "how" question.

Figure 2.23 A Myth from the Karok People

How Coyote Stole Fire

A long time ago, the Earth had no *Fire*. The Karok people, and all the other peoples of the world, were cold all through the winter and had no warming fires for their food. But Coyote knew that hidden in a cave far away was Fire. Because the Karoks had always been kind, never chasing him or killing Baby Coyote, Coyote decided to steal Fire for these sad people.

Coyote called a great council of the animals—Mountain Lion, Bear, Rabbit, Frog -- and spoke to them. "I need you to help me steal Fire from its cave and bring it to the Karok people who have always been your friend." "How have the Karok people been our friend?" asked Mountain Lion to Cyote. "Well," Cyote responded. "They never chase you from your mountain homes nor do they kill your cubs." "And why should I help the Karok people? Questioned Frog. Coyote answered, "Other people spoil the rivers and streams so frogs and fish can't live in them, but the Karok people always keep the water clean.

Bear and Rabbit also were pleased with Coyote's answers and all the animals asked how they could help.Coyote lined up the animals by size. "Mountain Lion, first. You can creep into the cave, grab Fire with your paws, put Fire on your back and race as fast as you can. Bear, you will be second. Mountain Lion will be hot and tired when you see him racing down the mountain. Be ready, grab Fire in your paws, and continue running through the woods.

Rabbit, you will be third and waiting behind a tree for Bear. Bear will throw you Fire and "quick as a bunny", you race to the stream where Frog will be on dry land. Frog you are last to catch Fire. Hop with all the strength of your two back legs to the teepees of the Karoks. I will alert them that you are coming and they will have gathered dry wood so that Fire can burn brighter and warmer. Now go Mountain Lion."

Each animal did its job, grateful to the Karoks for being so thoughtful—Mountain Lion, grabbing Fire, passing it to Bear, Bear passing it to Rabbit, and Rabbit passing it to Frog. When Frog arrived at the Karoks' teepees, Coyote was waiting. He had instructed the Indians to have a large mound of dry wood and as Frog made his last, long hop, Fire was thrown onto the wood and immediately blazed as never before.

Every Karok grabbed a piece of dry wood and lit another fire, till the whole land was bright and warm.

"Keep Fire going," announced Coyote, "and take care of the animals who help you"

And from that day to this, Coyote and all the other animals have been kept warm by Fire with the help of Karok people.

*Originally considered an independent stock, the **Karok** are now classed in a much larger linguistic connection known as the Hokan family.

Originally considered an independent stock, the **Karok** are now classed in a much larger linguistic connection known as the Hokan family.

Share Figure 2.24 "What is a Myth?" with your students. Then ask them to show how the story of Coyote fits the definition of a myth.

FIGURE 2.24 WHAT IS A MYTH? How does the story of Coyote fit the definition of a myth?

QUESTION	CATEGORY	CHARACTERISTICS
What is a myth? A myth is a	story that	1) explains a scientific idea in a non-scientific story 2) begins by asking "why" or "how" 3) often uses animals, gods, or make-believe creatures as characters 4) is usually related to a specific cultural group (ex. American Indians, Ancient Greece, African tribes or nations)

FIGURE 2.25 FRAME FOR WRITING A MYTH

> Imagine that you have lived a long time ago and are very curious about nature or human behavior. You keep asking "why" or "how" and when you can't find the answer you go to a group of wise people in your community with the question. They give you the answer and you record it in the language you know how to write. Here are some possible questions you might ask. Then write your answer using the characteristics of a myth. (You can also ask and answer your own "myth" question.)
>
> Why do the stars twinkle?   Why are the oceans salty?
>
> How did the world get to be round?   How did humans learn to speak?
>
> Why does the elephant have a trunk?   How did the dog get to be a person's best friend?

Who's Who In the Inventions and Understanding of Electricity?

Electricity -- The physical phenomena arising from the behavior of electrons and protons that is caused by the attraction of particles with opposite charges and the repulsion of particles with the same charge.

Imagine your community lit by candles and oil lamps, cooking over a fire, heating only through a fireplace, laundry done only by hand scrubbing, and dozens of other "inconveniences." Even today, there are parts of the world where this scenario exists. Because, without an understanding of electricity, humans had to depend of what was *visible* and possible to do only *by hand*.

The early Greeks, among others ancient people, had a vague understanding of an "invisible force" in the atmosphere, especially when lightning appeared to cause sparks and fire. But the in-depth understanding of what electricity is or does begins in the 18th century and becomes better known as a result of the curiosity and experiments of Benjamin Franklin. His curiosity is aroused in 1746, on a visit to Boston, when he saw some early experiments using electricity. Franklin had already been corresponding with a scientist in London named Peter Collinson and now he was motivated to try out some of his own ideas. Through his understanding that electricity was some "mysterious positive and negative force", he went on to develop a series of experiments that would set the stage for future scientists and more sophisticated experiments, among which were:

- making an electrical battery
- using an iron rod to bring electricity into his house
- sending a current through water to ignite alcohol
- "capturing" electricity by placing a key on a kite during an "electrical" storm

While Benjamin Franklin was one of the earliest experimenters with electricity, other scientists were also curious and throughout the 18th, 19th, and 20th centuries electrical experiments and electrical products changed the lives of countless humans throughout much of the world. Figure 2.26 is a Taxonomy of selected early scientists and inventors who provided us with electrical concepts and products that are common in every industrial society and changed the way humans live and work.

Following is Figure 2.26, a Taxonomy which students can use to research the accomplishments of contributors to sciences related to electricity. You will note that the students are asked to search for scientists of different backgrounds. For fun and expanded vocabulary, students can check on scientists who have become eponyms (ex. wattage/watts). Figure 2.27 *EPONYMS OF SPARK* get them started.

FIGURE 2.26-- TAXONOMY OF SELECTED SCIENTISTS AND INVENTORS RELATED TO ELECTRICITY

Gilbert, William (British) 1544-1603 - Scientist and physician, father of the science of electricity and magnetism.

Watt, James (Scottish) 1736 – 1819 - Inventor and mechanical engineer whose improvements to the Newcomen steam engine resulted in the early developments of the train as a major form of transportation.

Galvani, Luigi (Italian) 1737-1798 – Discovered the electrical basis of nerve impulses and the ideas that led to his great discovery of the intimate connection existing between magnetism and electricity and galvanism.

Volta, Alessandro (Italian) 1745 - 1827) - Known especially for the discovery of bioelectricity and the development of the first electric cell in 1800.

Ampere, Andre Marie (French) 1775-1836 - The first scientist to demonstrate that a magnetic field is generated when two parallel wires are charged with electricity and is one of the discoverers of electromagnetism.

Hans Oersted (Danish) 1777 –1851- A physicist and chemist who made additional contributions related to the force of electromagnetism.

Ohm, Georg Simon (German) 1789 -1854 - Ohm started his research with the recently invented *electrochemical cell*, and was able to define the relationship between voltage, current, and resistance known as Ohm's law, the true beginning of electrical circuitry and conduction.

Faraday, Michael (English) 1791 – 1867- The discoverer of electro-magnetic induction, electro-magnetic rotations, the magneto-optical effect, diamagnetism, field theory and the electric motor.

Joule, James Prescott (British) 1818-1889 - Formulated the law, known as Joule's law, of electric heating, which states that the amount of heat produced in a conductor of electricity is proportional to the resistance of the conductor and to the square of the current.

Edison, Thomas Alva (American) 1847-1931) - Many inventions such as the incandescent bulb, the phonograph and the motion picture.

Bell, Alexander Graham (American) 1847–1922 - Scientist, inventor, engineer and innovator who is credited with inventing the first telephone.

Tesla, Nikola 1856–1943 (Croatian) - Developer of resonant transformer circuit used to produce high voltage AC electricity for improved broadcast network communications.

Hertz, Heinrich (German) 1857 –1894) - German physicist who clarified and expanded the electromagnetic theory of light and demonstrated the existence of electromagnetic waves.

Deforest, Lee (American) 1873-1961 - Invented the audion, a vacuum tube device that could take a weak electrical signal and amplify it into a larger one and used from radios to televisions to the first computers.

Marconi, Guglielmo (Italian) 1874–1937 - Celebrated for his development of wireless telegraphy radio). In the field of electromagnetic waves he correlated and improved previous electric-related inventions.

FIGURE 2.27 EPONYMS* OF SPARK

Many words related to electricity have come from the scientists who expanded our knowledge of this subject. Here are the names of seven scientists whose names are now words. Find their names on the Internet and write the definition of the word that comes from their name (example: Volta – voltage)

Andre Ampere - ampere

Luigi Galvani – galvanize

Heinrich Hertz – hertz for electrical frequency

James Prescott Joule – joule

George Simon Ohm – ohm

James Watts – watts or wattage

Alessandro Volta – volts/voltage

*Eponym - a word based on or derived from a person's name, from the Greek "name of a person

Microscopes and Telescopes For Seeing the Infinitesimal and the Big Picture

> *... my work, which I've done for a long time, was not pursued in order to gain the praise I now enjoy, but chiefly from a craving after knowledge, which I notice resides in me more than in most other men. And therewithal, whenever I found out anything remarkable, I have thought it my duty to put down my discovery on paper, so that all ingenious people might be informed thereof.* Letter of June 12, 1716 from Anton van Leeuwenhoek (born in Delft, Holland October 1632, died 1723

We begin this section with an introduction to the lens grinder and eventually scientist, Anton van Leeuwenhoek, who, through his diligence and dedication, opened up the world of microscopic life, changing the view of his world and the history of biology.

Although the compound microscope had been invented about forty years before Leeuwenhoek was born, it was Leewenhoek's grinding lenses that eventually allowed him to build microscopes that magnified over 200 times, with clear and bright images. In addition, he had the curiosity to observe almost anything that he could under his lenses, and then carefully describe what he saw.

Here are two examples of his observations looking through his microscope:

September 7, 1674

"Passing just lately over this lake, . . . and examining this water next day, I found floating therein divers earthy particles, and some green streaks, spirally wound and orderly arranged, after the manner of the copper or tin worms.... The whole circumference of each of these streaks was about the thickness of a hair of one's head... all consisted of very small green globules joined together...."

December 25, 1702,

"In structure these little animals (ciliates) were fashioned like a bell, and at the round opening they made such a stir, that the particles in the water thereabout were set in

motion thereby... very gently moving, with outstretched bodies and straightened-out tails; yet in an instant... they pulled their bodies and their tails together, and no sooner had they contracted their bodies and tails, than they began to stick their tails out again very leisurely...."

Thus, this lens grinder and scientist would be the forerunner of the microcosmic world that would irrevocably alter our knowledge of invisible life on Earth. The lens, this magical piece of glass, not only magnified the unseen, but enlarged the "seen", when it became telescopic, initially causing religious and social disruption by forcing humans to change their cosmic views. Eventually, however, we had no choice but to realize that our Earth revolved around the Sun and the Universe was far greater than any Earthling had possibly imagined (see Sobol on *Galileo's Daughter*, 1999 and Primack & Abrams, *The View From the Center of the Universe, 2006)*. Technology had arrived, but its future course was yet to be seen.

To engage your students in this Epoch of Change, we have set up a *Dual Taxonomy* (Figure 2.28) of selected biologists for whom the **microscope** expanded our knowledge of the invisible and selected astronomers for whom the **telescope** expanded our knowledge of the vastness of our skies and beyond. Figure 2.29 illustrates the strategy of *Personifications and Interactions* in which a biologist and astronomer correspond each telling of how their "instrument" added scientific knowledge. You can use these two figures as samples for getting started on student research related to these two great instruments.

FIGURE 2.28 SAMPLING OF BIOLOGISTS AND ASTRONOMERS

BIOLOGISTS AND MICROSCOPES	ASTRONOMERS AND TELESCOPES
Martinus Beijerinck (1851–1931), Dutch microbiologist and botanist at the Technical University at Delft, the Netherlands, put forth his concepts that viruses were small and infectious. Is known as the discoverer of viruses.	**Benjamin Banneker** (1731-1806), an African American mathematician and amateur astronomer who made projections for solar and lunar eclipses and computed ephemeredes (tables of the locations of celestial bodies) for an almanac using a simple telescope.
Jules Bordet (1870–1961), Belgian immunologist and microbiologist, winner of the 1919 Nobel Prize in Medicine for his discovery of the complement system in the immune system.	**Galileo Galilei** (1564-1642), Italian, through his use of the telescope, performed observations, experiments, and mathematical analyses in astronomy; discovered mountains and craters on the moon, the phases of Venus, and the four largest satellites of Jupiter: Io, Europa, Callisto, and Ganymede.
Emmett W. Chappelle (1925 -) American, bacteriologist and chemist, discovered a method for detecting bacteria in water, food, and body fluids, recognized as one of the 100 most distinguished African American scientists.	**William K. Hartmann** (1939-) American, co-developed the most widely accepted theory of the formation of the Moon (from the collision of a giant planetismal with the Earth at the close of the planet-forming period of the solar system)
Gerty Radnitz Cori (1957–1986), born in Prague, Czech Republic, biochemist, winner of numerous awards, including the Nobel Prize, for her work in hormones and their effects on human growth.	**Ejnar Hertzsprung** 1873-1967 Danish, by studying star clusters, independently discovered the relationship between absolute magnitude and spectral types of stars, now called a Hertzsprung-Russell diagram (or H-R diagram).

Francis Crick (1916–2004), British, one of the discoverers of the structure of the DNA molecule and a neurobiologist winner of won the 1962 Gardener Foundation Award, the 1972 Royal Society's Royal Medal, and the 1976 Royal Society's Copley Medal.

Ochoa, Severo (1905–1993), Spanish born biochemist. With Arthur Kornberg, he received the 1959 Nobel Prize in medicine for the synthesis of ribonucleic acid (RNA).

Bei Shizhang (1903 – 2009) Chinese biologist, pioneer of Chinese cytology, embryology and the founder of Chinese biophysics. He was considered the "Father of Chinese Biophysics".

Yalow, Rosalyn Sussman, (1921-), American .developed a process, called radioimmunoassay to detect mere traces of biological substances in blood and other fluids. Awarded the 1977 Nobel Prize in Physiology

Stephen W. Hawking (1942-) British British combined general relativity with quantum theory to predict that black holes should emit radiation and evaporate.

Maria Mitchell 1818–89, American astronomer, discovered a comet (1847 VI) not far from Polaris. First woman to be elected (1848) to the American Academy of Arts and Sciences. With a *5-in. Alvan Clark refractor,* she expanded her studies of sunspots, planets, and nebulae.

Vera Rubin 1928-
American measured rotation curves for distant galaxies and ultimately concluded that 90% or more of the universe is made of invisible dark matter

Carl Sagan 1934-1996
American leader in the search for extraterrestrial intelligence; contributed to space missions to explore Mars and the outer planets; warned that all-out nuclea rwar could lead to a ``nuclear winter''

FIGURE 2.29 - PERSONIFICATIONS AND INTERACTIONS – BIOLOGIST WRITES TO ASTRONOMER AND VICE-VERSA

Here is an example of an imaginary letter written by biologist Emmett W. Chappelle to Vera Rubin, astronomer.

Instructions for your letter.

- Use this imaginary letter of Emmett Chappelle written to Vera Rubin, a renowned astronomer as a model for your own letter.

- Pair up with a partner, with one of you being a biologist of accomplishment whom you have found out about on the Internet or other source, and the other partner being an accomplished astronomer.

- Now write to each other including your:

    specific investigation and findings

    contribution to scientific knowledge

    awards or special recognition

Sample Letter (Note: Make up an address where you might be writing from and the approximate date of you writing. Don't worry if you and your science colleague are from very different periods of time.)

Emmett W. Chappelle, Ph.D.
222 Bell Road
Phoenix, AZ 85032
Dr. Vera Rubin
Carnegie Institution
Washington, DC

October 18, 1970

Dear Dr. Rubin:

I recently read of your extraordinary accomplishments in the field of astronomy and your specific discovery of dark matter in the Universe. As a biologist and chemist, I believe we have much to share and I would like to tell you something about my work and hopefully hear from you about your interests and discoveries.

Most recently, I have been involved in finding ways to determine the health of forest vegetation. As a scientist you undoubtedly realize that preserving the growth of plants in forests is essential to having a healthy environment. The health of plants is directly related to photosynthesis, the process by which plants use the energy from sunlight to chemically convert this energy to form the green pigment called chlorophyll. The photosynthetic process is necessary to release the oxygen that we absolutely must have to stay alive. By using a special process called fluorescence through the aid of a laser instrument, I was able to monitor the amount of photosynthesis that is occurring in forests. Plants that were showing loss of photosynthesis could be rescued and brought back to health and thereby we could preserve the oxygen system so necessary for all life.

As a result of my work, I was honored to receive many awards, one of which is the NASA's Exceptional Achievement Medal.

I would like to hear about your incredible work, Dr. Rubin, and some of the awards you have won. I look forward to an exciting exchange of ideas and an increase of my knowledge about the Universe.

Very sincerely,

Emmett Chappelle, Ph.D.

The Digital Age for Global Communication

In the final decades of the 20th century a singular, yet on-going event, occurred that is perhaps the most significant of all the changes to affect education—the arrival and spread of digital technology. The vast majority of our students are growing up immersed in a digital world of computers, cell phones, music players, televisions and cameras that can all be connected and shared via a global internet. It is inevitable that as a result of their comfort with and sheer amount of time spent using digital technology, students think and process information not only differently than students from previous generations but differently from the adults who teach them (Prensky, 2001). How can classroom teachers meet this challenge and more importantly engage with students using the technology available?

Stories and storytelling have been used by all cultures throughout all of history as a means to share important knowledge as well as to entertain. We still use stories today and engaging students in storytelling is a powerful way for them to exercise creativity as they learn about themselves and the world around them.

Enough research has been done and continues to be done, Hibbing and Rankin-Erikson (2003) and Boster, Meyer, Toberto, & Inge (2002) showing that the use of multimedia during instruction helps students learn and retain new information. Digital Storytelling can provide educators with a powerful tool to use in their classrooms either in creating their own digital stories to introduce new concepts, enhance lessons, or to turn over to the students. Student produced digital stories can be in response to an inquiry project, or to demonstrate use of such creative academic talents as organization, writing, presenting and of course working with visual images to enhance communication.

In **Figure 2.30, Who's Who in the Digital Story,** we have cited the names of the inventors and developers as part of our Who's Who strategy in the Planning Wheel (see Figure 1.1). We suggest, as an ongoing project, students research the history of computer pioneers and innovators who have changed the way we live, work, and think and add to this list, bringing it as up to date as possible. At the end of this figure, we have provided Figure 2.31, a *Frame* titled **Person of Accomplishment** (Rothstein, Rothstein, & Lauber, 2007) to guide your students in writing a focused article on a computer developer.

FIGURE 2.30 WHO'S WHO IN THE DIGITAL STORY

1622 - **William Oughtred** invents the **slide rule**. This first one was circular.
1623- **Wilhelm Schickard** designs the first known mechanical calculator, the "**Calculating Clock**" to multiply large numbers.
1642 - **Blaise Pascal** invents an adding machine, which he calls the **Pascaline**. It could perform addition and subtraction, but it was too expensive to be practical and only Pascal could keep it working.
1666 - **Samuel Morland** builds a **mechanical calculator** that will add and subtract.
1674- **Gottfried Leibnez**, the man to honor for the invention of calculus, uses a stepped cylindrical gear to build his "*Stepped Reckoner*" which will both add and multiply; also introduces binary mathematics.
1774- **Phillip-Malthus Hahn** builds and sells a small number of calculating machines, which are accurate to 12 digits.
1777 - The third **Earl of Stanhope** invents a **multiplying calculator.**
1804 - **Joseph-Marie Jacquard** invents an automated loom, which uses **punched cards** to reproduce complex patterns.
1820 - The first mass-produced calculating machine developed by Thomas **de Colmar's Arithmometer** is marketed and continues in use for many years.
1822 - **Charles Babbage** begins work on the **Difference Engine.**

1829 - The first **typewriter** is patented by **William Austin Burt**. It's slow and clumsy, but it's the first writing machine.
1838 - **Samuel Morse** demonstrates the principle of the telegraph.
1840 - **Ada**, **Countess** of **Lovelace**, (Lord Byron's daughter) suggests to Babbage that he use the binary system. She writes programs for his analytical engine, becoming the world's **first programmer.**
1850's – **George Boole** develops **Boolean Logic** which will one day become the basis for computer logic.
1876 - **Alexander Graham Bell** invents the telephone.
1890 - **Dr. Herman Hollerith** introduces the first electro-mechanical punched-card data processing machine. It is used to compile information from the 1890 US census.
1892 - **Burroughs** produces the **first adding machine** with a **printer.**
1901 - **Guglielmo Marconi** sends the first transatlantic wireless message.
1906- **William DeForest** invents the **vacuum tube.**
1919- Two American physicists, **Eccles** and **Jordan**, invent the **flip-flop** circuit, which will be necessary for high-speed electronic calculating.
1930 - **Vannevar Bush** builds the **differential analyzer** at M.I.T.
1936- **Konrad Zuse** applies for a patent on his mechanical memory.
1936 - **Alan Turing** publishes *On Computable Numbers* which lays a theoretical foundation for computer principles.

CHAPTER TWO EPOCHS OF CHANGE AND EDUCATIONAL IMPLICATIONS

1937 - **George Stibitz** builds his **Model K**, which demonstrates the feasibility of mechanizing binary math.
1939 - **John Atanasoff** begins work on his **ABC computer.**
1939 - **Howard Aiken** begins work on the **Harvard Mark 1.**
1940 - **Konrad Zuse** introduces his **Z1,** the first programmable calculating machine to use the binary system. It is used to solve complex engineering equations.
1940 - **George Stibitz and Samuel Williams** complete the Complex Number Computer, later known as the Bell Labs Model 1.
1941 - **Alan Turing, M.H.A. Newman** and **Tommy Flowers** complete work on the Colossus, the first all-electronic calculating machine. It is used during WWII to break German codes.
1942 - **John Mauchly** and **J. Presper Eckert** propose a digital electronic version of Vannevar Bush's differential analyzer.
1943 - **Howard Aiken** and staff at IBM's Endicott Labs complete the Harvard Mark 1, an automatic digital sequence-controlled computer.
1946 - **Herman Goldstine** invents flowcharts.
1947- **William Shockley, John Bardeen and Walter Brattain** invent the transistor.
1949 - **An Wang** develops magnetic core memory.
1949 - **Jay Forrester** and his team at MIT develop the first real-time computer.
1951- **William Shockley** invents the junction transistor.
1952 - **Jay Forester** develops magnetic memory at M.I.T.

1952 - **Grace Murray Hopper** develops A-O, the first program compiler.
1954- **Gordon Teal** develops transistors based on silicon.
1956 - **John Bardeen, Walter Brattain**, and **William Shockley** win the Nobel Prize in physics for their work on the transistor.
1957 - **John Backus** develops the FORTRAN programming language.
1958 - **Jack St. Clair Kilby** and **Robert Noyce** develop the first integrated circuit (IC) or chip, which is a collection of miniature transistors.
1959 - **Robert Noyce** builds an integrated circuit based on silicon, with metal conductors, transistors and resistors.
1959 - **John McCarthy** develops the programming language LISP.
1960 - **Ken Olsen** introduces the PDP-1, the first computer with a keyboard and a monitor. The first mass produced minicomputer is sold at the unheard-of low price of $20.0000.
1960 - **Paul Baran** develops the packet-switching principle for data communication.
1961- **Fernando Corbato** develops a way for computer users to share computer time.
1961 - **George C. Devolo** patents the first robotic manufacturing device used to automate manufacturing TV tubes.
1962 - **Ivan Sutherland** creates a graphics system called Sketchpad.
1962 - **Steve Russell**, grad student at MIT develops the first video game.
1962 - **Joseph Weizenbaum** develops Eliza, a computer program that simulates the responses of a psychiatrist.

1963 - Douglas Engelbart receives a patent on the mouse-pointing device for computers.

1963 - Lofti Zadeh begins work on fuzzy logic at UC Berkeley.

1964 - John Kemeny and Thomas Kurtz at Dartmouth College develop the programming language BASIC.

1967- Jack Kilby, John Merryman and **James VanTassel** develop the first four-function hand-held calculator.

1969 - Dennis Ritchie and **Kenneth Thompson** begin work on the UNIX operating system Intel and announce a 1 KB RAM chip which has a significantly larger capacity **than any previously produced memory chip.**

1969 - William Gates and **Paul Allen**, calling themselves the "Lakeside Programming Group" sign an agreement with Computer Center Corporation to report bugs in PDP-10 software, in exchange for computer time.

1969 - Gary Starkweather demonstrates the use of a laser beam with the xerography process to create a laser printer.

1970 - Gilbert Hyatt files the first basic patent on the microprocessor.

1971- Tom Hoff develops the first mass-produced microprocessor, the Intel 4004, which can process four bits of data simultaneously at a rate 60,000 instructions per second and has its own arithmetic logic unit.

1971 - Nolan Bushnell invents the videogame "Pong" and becomes the father of videogames.

1971 - John V. Blankenbaker designs the first microcomputer kit.

1971 - Nicklaus Wirth develops PASCAL, a structured programming language.

1972 - Alain Colmerauer develops the Porlog language at University of Marseilles.
1973 - Steve Wozniak begins to build "Blue Boxes", tone generators to make free long-distance calls, and sells them in his dorm at Berkeley.
1974 -Steven Jobs and **Stephen Wozniak** start building computers in the Jobs' family garage; the start of what would become Apple.
1975 -Ed Roberts, considered the father of the personal computer, designs the Altair 8800.
1975 -William Gates and **Paul Allen** offer to build a BASIC compiler for MITS which is to be the start of what will become Microsoft.
1976 -Gary Killdall starts Digital Research and introduces the CP/M operating system.
1978- Dan Bricklin and **Bob Frankston** write VisiCalc, the first electronic spreadsheet.
1982 - Mitchell Kapor designs Lotus 1-2-3.
1982 - John Warnock develops PostScript.
1983 - Michael Dell begins building computers in his college dorm room.
1989- Seymour Cray begins to develop the Cray 3.
Add what has happened since!!

FIGURE 2.31 PERSON OF ACCOMPLISHMENT FRAME

Directions: Use this Frame to write a summary biographical statement about a person who contributed to our use and knowledge of the computer and other digital products. Use the Internet and any other sources to find information about the person you are writing about. You can also expand this Frame into a full biographical piece.

In the year (or During the years)_____ (Name of Person)
_____ (developed, invented, began)
_____. He or She always
wanted/hoped/experimented _____.

To accomplish this goal (goals, dreams)
_____

As a result of his/her dedication and determination, _____

CHAPTER 3 - STUDENT-CENTERED TEACHING AND LEARNING

Scientific observation has established that education is not what the teacher gives; education is a natural process spontaneously carried out by the human individual, and is acquired not by listening to words but by experiences upon the environment. The task of the teacher becomes that of preparing a series of motives of cultural activity, and then refraining from obtrusive interference. [As servants of the child] human teachers can only help the great work that is being done.

Doing so, they will be witness to the unfolding of the human soul and to the rising of a New Human who will not be the victim of events, but will have the clarity of vision to direct and shape the future of human society.

Maria Montessori (1946) Education for a New World

This chapter offers strategies that are central to the *needs of all students*, particularly in the 21st century, both as we already know it and as best as we can envision its future. Creating an environment where students are empowered to become self-directed learners and have every opportunity to reach their highest potential is essentially defining excellence in education for ALL learners. It becomes of paramount importance to provide quality education conducive to the learners needs not necessarily confined to the paradigm of what we have come to know in the past as the classroom. By merging the physical classroom with the now-available immersive classrooms we offer two segments:

- Models of Learning for All Learners
- Finding Your Niche, Building Your Interests

These segments are both print and computer connected and are designed to provide a seamless relationship between the two media, one of which is this book that serves as the guide or pathway to the technological richness that will give 21st century learners the knowledge and skills they need to have for fulfilling economically successful lives. You are likely to find that the "print" has time-stability, meaning that what we *say* has a relatively long *shelf* life, but that our technological references and suggestions are on wings, quickly outdated just as you are getting to know or use them. Nevertheless, old-fashioned book print (slow, but stable) and technological print (fast, but ephemeral) can still provide us with knowledge and is what we currently need to be educated. So we'll begin where we believe we have to begin—with Models of Learning that have stood the test of time and research and point to success for all learners.

MODELS OF LEARNING

> *...I argue that there is persuasive evidence for the existence of several relatively autonomous human intellectual competences, hereafter known as "human intelligences"....[and] that these are relatively independent of one another....(Gardner, 1983 p.xxxi)*

In 1983, Howard Gardner began his book *Frames of the Mind* with a "Note on Human Potential" (xxxi) and cited three studies. One was his own work, which examined "human potential which draws ...on the biological sciences and findings about the *development and use of knowledge in different cultures"* (our italics, xxxii). The second study is from Israel Scheffler's *Of Human Potential*, which relates to "philosophical aspects of the concept of potential" (xxxii) and "offers systematic reflections on policy and the education of policy makers" (xxxii). Finally there is the work of Robert A. Levine and Merry I. White, *The Cultural Basis of Educational Development*, which emphasizes the "crucial role of cultural factors in the progress of human development... [and] offers new models for development based on the social anthropology of the lifespan and the social history of family and school" (xxxii).

Gardner, in the same introduction, argues for diversity and international dialogue in the educational communities which would "create a new multidisciplinary environment for understanding human potential" (xxxii), a goal that has yet to be reached, but has the possibilities of being reachable with new visions, the potential of technology, and the belief that every child is endowed with intellectual competences.

So with Gardner's prescient plea in 1983 for developing human potential, we are modestly offering our own and researched models of teaching and learning that can bring all students into the global arena of knowledge, inter-lingual communication, and the joy of sharing their lives and spirit with fellow humans everywhere through the expanding tools of the current century.

In naming this segment *Models of Learning*, we took the risk of assuming that all of us involved in schools know what this term means. But then, thanks to the quick access to the Internet, we came across the website below and found ourselves faced with a plethora of information that now needs to be sorted out and made useful, not only to those directly involved in the classroom, but to all those other "educators" who serve as decision-makers and are likely to have their own concepts (and opinions) of what the models are and which of these models they want implemented.

So before we begin with our own opinions and concepts we refer you to the theories listed in http://www.learning-theories.com (retrieved November, 2013) for your own information, and have taken the liberty of drawing from those which we (currently) believe have best served large numbers of students or have the greatest potential. With this selection, we can look to ways of getting connected with 21st century learners embarking on their paths of learning, assisted by the continuous development of technological tools. For each of the models we have selected, we have added a specific learning strategy (or strategies) which you can try and build on and to which we have added Internet references.

Learning Theories and Models

http://www.learning-theories.com (retrieved December, 2010)

The above cited website provides an index of learning theories, grouped into the categories of:

Behaviorism Cognitivism, Constructivism Design-Based Humanism

For this book, we have drawn from *Behaviorism and Constructivism,* as two examples of Learning Models, which we believe, are particularly valuable for student learning. However, we encourage your own research of other models in order to find those points that resonate for you and we plan in the future to offer strategies related to them.

Social Learning Theory -- We have selected, as one model for 21st century learners, Bandura's *Social Learning Theory* (1986) which states that people learn from one another via observation, imitation, and modeling all of which encompass attention, memory, and motivation. We can assume that every teacher wishes for a classroom where students attend to the lessons, remember what was taught, and are motivated to move ahead! But since this *nirvana* of classroom behavior is more the ideal than the reality, the means for achieving this goal are heavily dependent on teacher modeling that motivates students to observe and imitate.

In the best of all possible classrooms, the teacher, as model, must harness attention, have strategies for retention, foster reproduction of positive behavior, and constantly promote motivation. The ideas and theories of Bandura are also related to related to Vygotsky's *Social Development Theory* (1978) and to Lave's *Situated Learning* (1988, 1990), which also emphasize the importance of social learning. So how can culturally responsive teaching and the tools of technology enhance social learning and promote the development of high-level learning which is dependent on memory and motivation?

The advancement from "teacher as lecturer and dispenser of knowledge" to some acceptance of "social learning" in school began (at least in part) when the classroom desks, which had been bolted into the schoolroom floor, became movable. This change began somewhere in the 1950's and only gradually did students get to move out of "rows" into varied groupings. Yet even today, sixty plus years later, there are "rows" of students, minus the bolts. But the rows are finally becoming obsolete and new paradigms of teaching and learning are rapidly forming assisted by hand-held devices such as *i-pods* and *i-pads*, blogging, text-messaging, e-mailing, "computer-chatting," "tweeting", surfing and downloading, among current tech tools, with new ones on the horizon.

We begin with the exploration and use of text-messaging as an inevitable use in the classroom and within the model of *social learning*. First, students are constantly developing new structures for this "communication" system. Second, they are the experts both in the creation of text styles and in their technological capabilities--far "ahead" of the adults in their lives. And finally, they are just doing it, in their private lives and in school. We begin with possible classroom "lessons" that can be incorporated with text messaging and how can we help students expand their language skills and knowledge through this unique medium that is currently the extension of a cell phone.

The Literacy of Real-Time Text Based Communication

With the popularity and extensive use of real-time text-based communications, such as that used in *Twitter, social networking, instant messaging, e-mail, online gaming services, chat rooms, discussion boards*, and *mobile phone text messaging*, people of all ages are engaged in exercising literacy that uses language tailored to the immediacy and compactness of these new communication media.

Abbreviated messages have been around for a long time, such as ASAP (as soon as possible) and began most noticeably with the invention of the electric telegram by Samuel F.B. Morse in 1837 with a series of dots and dashes and short word messages that were developed to keep down the costs of the telegrams. Today we have an evolution of language that is growing exponentially, mostly through the creation of our youth. The following link provides a listing of more than 1300 text abbreviations and their definitions, with more to come.

To get started, we begin as an example of bringing history into modern times with Figure 3.1, which asks the student to revise the letters of Abigail Adams to John Adams into Text Message format. This activity is based on the Planning Wheel strategy of Personifications and Interactions and lends itself particularly well to social studies. If you (and your students) like this activity, you can also ask each student to compose his/her own message about a topic or idea you are teaching and share it with another classmate. Or you can ask the students to compose their own text messages, post them on a wall or *SmartBoard,* and individually reply. Students can also come up with ideas for appropriate use of texting in the classroom while learning their "academics".

Figure 3.1 Letters Between Abigail Adams and John Adams 1776

In 1776 Abigail Adams wrote to her husband John who was a delegate from Massachusetts, attending the historic convention demanding independence for the American Colonies from the British king. In this historic letter, Abigail Adams pleads for including the "ladies" in the demand for freedom and equality.

Revise these historic letters into 21st Century Text Messaging. You can use your own text message knowledge or search the Internet for a TM glossary. You can also make some changes in the letter to include more TM terms.

ORIGINAL LETTERS – 1776	TEXT MESSAGE LETTERS ADAPTED FOR THE 21st CENTURY WITH BOLDED ADDITIONS AND CHANGES

CHAPTER THREE STUDENT – CENTERED TEACHING AND LEARNING

MARCH 31, 1776 **ABIGAIL ADAMS TO JOHN ADAMS**	MARCH 31, 20 TEXT MESSAGE
"I long to hear that you have declared an independency. And, by the way, in the new code of laws, which I suppose it will be necessary for you to make, I desire you would remember the ladies and be more generous and favorable to them than your ancestors. "Do not put such unlimited power into the hands of the husbands. "Remember, all men would be tyrants if they could. If particular care and attention is not paid to the ladies, we are determined to foment a rebellion, and will not hold ourselves bound by any laws in which we have no voice or representation. "That your sex are naturally tyrannical is a truth so thoroughly established as to admit of no dispute; but such of you as wish to be happy willingly to give up -- the harsh tide of master for the more tender and endearing one of friend. "Why, then, not put it out of the power of the vicious and the lawless to use us with cruelty and indignity with impunity? "Men of sense in all ages abhor those customs which treat us only as the (servants) of your sex; regard us then as being placed by Providence under your protection, and in imitation of the Supreme	"I long **2** hear that **u** have declared an independency. And, **btw**, in the new code of laws which I suppose it will **b** necessary for **u 2** make, **ayec** I desire **u** would remember the ladies and **b** more generous and favorable **2** them than your ancestors. It's time to be **14AA41**. "Do not put such unlimited power into the hands of the husbands. "**Bme,** all men would **b** tyrants if they could. **Bs**, if particular care and attention is not paid **2** the ladies, we are determined **2** foment a rebellion, and will not hold ourselves bound by any laws in which we have no voice or representation. "That your sex are naturally tyrannical is a truth so thoroughly established as **2** admit of no dispute; but such of **u** as wish **2 b** happy willingly **2** give up the harsh tide of master **4** the more **10der** and **n**dearing **141** of friend. Why, then, not put it out of the power of the vicious and the lawless **2** use us with cruelty and **indigni-t** with **impuni-t?** "Men of **¢** in all ages abhor those customs which treat us only as the (servants) of your sex; regard us then as **b-ing** placed by Providence under your protection, and

Being make use of that power only for our happiness."

NOW REVISE THESE LETTERS USING WHATEVER TEXT SYMBOLS YOU KNOW. YOU CAN MODIFY THE LETTER IF YOU WISH, BUT KEEP THE SAME IDEAS BETWEEN ABIGAIL AND JOHN.

APRIL 14, 1776

JOHN ADAMS TO ABIGAIL ADAMS

"As to your extraordinary code of laws, I cannot but laugh. "We have been told that our struggle has loosened the bonds of government everywhere; that children and apprentices were disobedient; that schools and colleges were grown turbulent; that Indians slighted their guardians, and negroes grew insolent to their masters.

"But your letter was the first intimation that another tribe, more numerous and powerful than all the rest, were grown discontented. "This is rather too coarse a compliment, but you are so saucy, I won't blot it out.

"Depend upon it, we know better than to repeal our masculine systems. Although they are in full force, you know they are little more than theory. We dare not exert our power in its full latitude. We are obliged to go fair and softly, and, in practice, you

in imitation of the **Supreme B-ing** make use of that power only **4** our happiness."

I **app u** so much and only ask that **u** please do this **asap wnsa**.

Lemeno what u think. GG

LOLO - Abigail

Glossary For Above Changes:

btw – by the wayzxx

ayec – at your earliest convenience

app - appreciate

asap – as soon as possible

141A41 – one for all, all for one

bme – by my experience

bs – be sure

wsna – with no strings attached.

¢ - cents/sense

gg- gotta go

know we are the subjects.

"We have only the name of masters, and rather than give up this, which would completely subject us to the despotism of the petticoat, I hope General Washington and all our brave heroes would fight."

MAY 7, 1776

<u>**ABIGAIL ADAMS TO JOHN ADAMS**</u>

"I cannot say that I think you are very generous to the ladies; for, whilst you are proclaiming peace and good-will to men, emancipating all nations, you insist upon retaining an absolute power over wives.

"But you must remember that arbitrary power is like most other things which are very hard, very liable to be broken; and, notwithstanding all your wise laws and maxims, we have it in our power, not only to free ourselves, but to subdue our masters, and without violence, throw both your natural and legal authority at our feet."

CHAPTER THREE STUDENT – CENTERED TEACHING AND LEARNING

Figure 3.2 has Harriet Tubman "texting" Sojourner Truth, with Sojourner responding. The task of the student is to revise the correspondence into standard spelling.

Figure 3.2 Harriet Tubman Texts Sojourner Truth, with Sojourner Responding. Revise the correspondence into standard spelling, adding more information if you can. Following these letters is a summary of the major events of Harriet Tubman's life and Sojourner Truth's life as they might have written them, with a follow-up activity.

Sojourner Truth Responds to Harriet Tubman by Text Message	**Revise Into Standard Spelling or Revise Letter and Add More Information from Sojourner to Harriet if you can.**
Dear Harriet: Dear Harriet: I know from your letter that we will **BFF**. **BION** I already have a plan for a **CTA**. When men say that a woman always needs a HH, I say "I am a woman" and that you are not **BTM** and that women and men are **4ever** equal and in **2ne** with each other's needs. **IMO**, which I know is also **IYO**, we should **POAHF**, **T☺T**, remember that **TIAD** and **TILIS**: If the 1st woman ever made was strong enough to **TTWUD** all alone, she ought to be able to get it **RSU** up again. **TA** and **KIT** Sojourner **TM Abbreviations:**	(For use by students)

BFF – best friends forever

BION – believe it or not

CTA – call to action

HH – helping hand

BTM – better than me

IMO – in my opinion

IYO – in your opinion

POAHF – put on a happy face

T☺T - think happy thoughts

TIAD – tomorrow is another day

TILIS – tell it like it is

TTWUD – turn the world upside down

RSU – right side up

TA – thanks again

KIT – keep in touch

Summary of Events in the Life of Harriet Tubman as she might have told it.

I am an African-African woman who was born into slavery in Dorchester County, Maryland. I was sold to many masters, and each one made me work from early morning to late at night. Often I was beaten with metal weights when my masters thought I wasn't working hard enough. In 1849 I escaped to Philadelphia where I met some abolitionists who would later help me rescue fellow slaves from slave states and guide them to freedom in free states. I was able to make thirteen missions and save the lives of at least seventy slaves in a system that became known as the Underground Railroad. We would travel by night and in extreme secrecy.

People began to call me "Moses" like the leader of the early Israelites who led his enslaved people out of Egypt. I was very proud to have this name. In 1850 the United States government passed the Fugitive Slave Law that said that an escaped slave belongs to her or his master and had to be returned. So I now had to make sure that slave fugitives would get to Canada where they would be safe from this law.

Summary of Events in the Life of Sojourner Truth as she might have told it.

I was one of thirteen children born in 1821 to James and Elizabeth Baumfree on an estate owned by a Dutch landowner named Colonel Hardenburgh located in the town of Esopus, New York. I was named Belle and for the first nine years of my life I spoke Dutch. When I was nine years old I was sold, along with a flock of sheep, to John Neely who was cruel and harsh and often beat me with a bundle of rods. I kept being sold and each time my life became more difficult. I was now married and had five children, but of course, the children belonged to my masters.

In 1826, I escaped with my daughter Sophia, but I had no choice but to leave my other children behind. I found my way to the home of Isaac and Maria Van Wagener, abolitionists, who took my baby and me into their home. In 1827 New York State passed the Emancipation Act and I was now a free woman. I was lucky to be able to move to

> New York City and work at jobs that paid me small wages. I believed that I had a mission in life to help other slaves, especially women, and after many years of hard work, I found my *calling* and changed my name to Sojourner Truth. I would preach about abolition, pacifism, religious tolerance, and the rights of women. In 1851, I attended the Women's Rights Convention in Akron, Ohio where I delivered my speech that later became known as "Ain't I a Woman".
>
> **With a partner, find two other women of history who would have a reason to share their lives. Each of you now writes in the voice of the woman you have selected. You can also set up your story as a letter.**

Extensions of *Bandura's Social Learning Through Classroom Activities*

A culturally responsive classroom means a classroom where learning is personalized and shared. Worksheets and textbook exercises are designed to be "solo" activities requiring students, for the most part, to work silently and then "hand-in" their work for teachers to grade and evaluate. The most *social learning* component of these activities is having the teacher ask students for the answers and hoping that the "silent students" are paying attention. We'd like to offer activities which will not only socialize and personalize your curriculum, but will develop research and communication skills.

Begin by having students write what they know or what they have learned to a fellow student and ask, in their writing, for information in return. Below is Figure 3.3 with an example for social learning of writing using the Metacognition Framework from the Planning Wheel and fully explained in *Writing As Learning*, Rothstein, Rothstein, & Lauber, Chapter 4).

Figure 3.3. Writing What You Know About to a Friend and Classmate. Use the Frame to write about a topic you know something about. The Frame is a model and you can change the topic to something that you are an expert on.

Dear _____

Today Mr. or Ms. taught us how to make a bar graph showing _____

I now know that we use a bar graph to _____

I also know that a bar graph can _____

One idea I have for using this kind of graph is to _____

Here is an example of what I have created: _____

Please tell me if you understand what I have done. Then write back to me and tell me what you know about these graphs and how you are using them.

Thanks so much.

Your friend and classmate,

Another form of learning and responding through social interaction is having the students create a dialogue between two characters either from the same book or story or from two stories from the same genre. For example, Figure 3.4 illustrates a dialogue between *Little Red Riding (LRRH)* and *Snow White (SW)* on their experiences of being alone in the woods. After the students have read this dialogue, have them create their own dialogue with two characters from a story they know well.

Figure 3.4. A Dialogue Between *Little Red Riding (LRRH)* and *Snow White (SW)* On Their Experiences of Being Alone in the Woods. First, read this dialogue with a classmate and then, with that classmate, create your own dialogue between two characters from a book you have both read.

SETTING: THE EDGE OF A DEEP WOOD

LRRH – Good morning. You must be Snow White. I recognize you from a picture book I have.

SW – And you are Little Red. I read about you when I was eight years old. You had a very scary experience.

LRRH – And you did too. How did you ever find your way to the house of those Dwarfs?

SW - Well, I knew about the different paths in the woods because the Hunter who worked for my stepmother would take me with him sometimes on his hunting trips and show me how to recognize which paths went where. He even pointed to a path that he said led to the house of the Dwarfs. And how did you ever find your way with that tricky Wolf interfering?

LRRH –It was almost like what happened to you. My mother took me to Grandma's house almost every month, so when I went alone, I thought I knew my way.

SW – Then how was the Wolf able to trick you?

LRRH - Well, I was only seven years old--I'm now nine—so I listened to him when he explained a short cut. Of course you know, he took the real short cut and I almost got lost.

SW – Luckily, the Woodcutter must have heard your Grandma crying for help.

LRHH – Yes, he was a kind man and always listened for Grandma calling in case she was in danger. He saved her life and mine too.

SW – I was also lucky because, as you know, the Dwarfs were kind and gave me a place to stay away from my wicked stepmother.

LRHH – But they shouldn't have all gone out to work. Maybe one should have stayed with you each day.

SW – That's true. But I guess they didn't think that anyone would find their way to the dwarves house so deep in the woods.

LRRH – We're both lucky we were saved, you by the Dwarfs and I by the Woodcutter.

SW – I have to get back to the castle where the Prince is waiting for me, but I hope we meet again.

LRRH – And I'm on way again to Grandma, only this time I know my way and the Wolf will never fool me again.

SW - Take care and let's stay in touch.

LRRH – Yes, for sure.

Expanding Social Learning Theory Through the Power of Language

One of the great educational debates of our time centers around the *English Only* movement, a controversial idea that has been very divisive in establishing the curriculum for immigrant children who speak a language other than English. Without specifically commenting on the educational perspective of this position, we state our argument based on the history and structure of the English language which today is the most widely spoken and written language in history.

English is a *polyglot* which means that it is composed of layers of languages that include vocabulary from Celtic, German, Latin, French, Spanish, Italian, Yiddish, Chinese, Urdu among other tongues. Because English is language that has "traveled" widely, mostly because of the British and its extended empire, it has gathered words from around the world. American English continued the gathering from its indigenous population, erroneously called Indians, and continued to add words from its welcoming (at various times in history) peoples from Europe and eventually, albeit reluctantly, from Asia and Africa, and today from its neighbors to the south. So we are grateful to all of these places for giving us the widest varieties of food any culture has ever had, musical terms from Italians and African-Americans, cities and states with names from French, Spanish, and "Amer-Indian", as well as an expansive corpus of vocabulary terms for the sciences and mathematics, mainly from Greek and Latin.

To understand the effect of this polyglot of English, we have created an *English Only* trip across the United States. The places traveled in this trip are written in "English", meaning of Anglo-Saxon origin or that we recognize clearly as "English." The task for the students is to find the current "Non-English" term in current use. For example, *Baton Rouge* is *French* for "red stick," *Las Cruces* is *Spanish* for "the crosses, and *Mississippi* means "big river" in *Ojibway*. The activity begins with Figure 3.5, **An English Only Trip Through America** and a glossary of terms from French, Spanish, and Native American peoples.

CHAPTER THREE STUDENT – CENTERED TEACHING AND LEARNING

Figure 3.5- An English Only Trip Through America.

Here is a "story" of a trip through America in which the names of the places visited are written in **English and bolded,** meaning that the names have been translated from their original language (French, for example) into the *English* word. After you have read the story, find the current names of these words and list them on the Taxonomies below the story (example: *Bottom of the Lake* in English is *Fond du Lac* in French and the French name is what we use for this city in Wisconsin.) There is a Taxonomy for placing French, Spanish, and American Indian names. After you have completed the Taxonomies, you can check your answers in the Answer Key that follows.

My *English Only* Trip Through the United States

Last summer I decided to take a trip across the United States and visit many cities and states. I only knew the "English" names of these places, but these names were not on the maps. So I searched the Internet and luckily found the current names of these places. I'm inviting you to also find their original and current names in either French, Spanish, or from American Indian nations. Write the current name under the language column of the Taxonomy and its meaning in English. Example: Las Cruces (New Mexico), Spanish for *The Crosses*. The first name in the story of the trip is "*Clear Mountain*"(New Jersey), translated from the French "Montclair."

If you like this activity you can search for other geographic names from French, Spanish, and American Indian nations.

Here's my trip:

In July, my family and I got into our car and began our cross-country trip across the United States. We started from my hometown of *Clear Mountain* in New Jersey and headed for *Beautiful Fort*, North Carolina. After a few days we headed south to the state of *Flowers* and the town of *Sea View*. We also spent a few days in *The Beauty* and also in *Adventure*.

We now headed to *Safe Harbor* and then to *Beautiful Fountain* in the state of *Vegetation Gatherers*. Soon we were on our way to the state of *South Wind* and the city of *Red Earth*. We decided to head north to the states of *Land of Tomorrow* and *Tribe of Superior Men*. Our destinations in the last state were the cities of Garlic *Field, The Barn*, and *Prairie of the Rock*. Heading west, we reached *The Monks* in Iowa, and then moved on to *Bottom of the Lake* and *Lake Short Ears* in Wisconsin. When we got to the state of *Sky-Tinted Water*, we rested a while in *Lake Who Speaks* County before heading west to *The Crosses* and *Holy Faith* in New Mexico, and *The Meadows* in Nevada. We would soon be in California and travel on *The Kings Mountain*, starting in *Sacramento*, then on to *Saint Francis, Saint Joseph, The Angels, Kings Navy,* and *Modest*. We headed back east, making sure we would get to New Orleans and stopped in *Red Stick, Chestnut Tree, Beautiful Island, Paradise,* and *Good Earth*. Happy, but tired, we headed home back to *Clear Mountain*, and started planning our next English Only trip, which turned out to be a great idea. Not only did we see many states and beautiful lakes and cities, but also we now had learned the original names of Indian places and also the original names that came from the French and Spanish explorers.

	FRENCH PLACE NAMES AND THEIR MEANINGS	SPANISH PLACE NAMES AND THEIR MEANINGS	AMERICAN INDIAN PLACE NAMES AND THEIR MEANING
A			
B			
C			
D			
E			
F			
G			
H			
I			
J			

K			
L			
M	Montclair – Clear Mountain		
N			
O			
P			
Q			
R			
S			
T			
U			
V			
W			
X			
Y			
Z			

Answer Key: French names, Spanish names, and American Indian names

Clear Mountain - *Montclair* (New Jersey), French

Beautiful Fort – *Beaufort* (North Carolina), French

The Flowers- *Florida,* Spanish

Sea View – *Miramar* (Florida) Spanish

The Beauty – *La Belle* (Florida) French

Adventure – *Aventura* (Florida) Spanish

Safe Harbor – *Bon Secour* (Alabama) French

Beautiful Fountain – *Belle Fontaine* (Alabama) French

Vegetation Gatherers – *Alabama* Choctaw Indians

South Wind - *Kansas* Sioux Indians

Tribe of Superior Men – Illinois, Algonquian

Garlic Field – Chicago (Illinois) Algonquian

The Barn - La Grange (Illinois) French

Prairie of the Rock – Prairie du Rocher (Illinois) French

The Monks- Des Moines (Iowa) French

Bottom of the Lake - Fond du Lac (Wisconsin) French

Lake Short Ears - Lac Courte Oreilles – (Wisconsin) French

Sky-Tinted Water – (Minnesota) Dakota Indians

Lake Who Speaks – Lac Qui Parle (Minnesota) French

The Crosses – Las Cruces (New Mexico) Spanish

Holy Faith – Santa Fe I(New Mexico) Spanish

The Meadows – La Vegas (Nevada) Spanish

Kings Mountain – Monterey, (California) Spanish

Sacrament - Sacramento (California) Spanish

> Saint Francis – San Francisco (California) Spanish
>
> Saint Joseph – San Jose (California) Spanish
>
> The Angels – Los Angeles (California) Spanish
>
> Kings Navy – Marina del Rey (California) Spanish
>
> Modest – Modesto (California) Spanish
>
> Red Stick – Baton Rouge (Louisiana) French
>
> Chestnut Tree – Chataingner (Louisiana) French
>
> Beautiful Island - Belle Isle (Louisiana) French
>
> Paradis – Paradise (Louisiana) French
>
> Good Earth - Terrebonne (Louisiana) French
>
> Clear Lake - Montclair (New Jersey) French

Constructivist Theories – Our second learning model is based on *Constructivist Theories* which include the concepts and ideas from *Communities of Practice (Lave and Wenger, 1988, 1990), Discovery of Learning (Bruner, 1960, 1966), Social Development Theory (Vygotsky 1978),* and *The Case for Constructivist Classrooms* (Brooks and Brooks, 1999)   http://www.funderstanding.com/content/constructivism, (retrieved December 5, 2010)

Constructivism, a philosophy of learning, is founded on the premise that by reflecting on our experiences, we construct our own understanding of the world we live in. We generate our own "rules" and "mental models," in order to make sense of our experiences. It is through constructivist learning that we accommodate new experiences

(Jacqueline and Martin Brooks, *The Case for Constructivist Classrooms,* 1999). The major principles of Constructivism are cited below:

- Learning is a search for meaning
- Meaning requires understanding wholes as well as parts, which must be understood in the context of wholes and not on facts.
- Learning expands when students make connections between fact and concepts
- Analyzing, comparing, and predicting foster high-level learning
- The purpose of learning is to construct meaning, not just memorize the "right" answers or state someone else's meaning.
- Hands-on problem-solving activates prior knowledge
- Open-ended questions bring about extensive student dialogue
- Learning is a social endeavor
- Assessment is based broad-based student learning rather than standardized testing and rigid grading systems

We would guess that most teachers and others in education would agree with these principles of learning, yet often withdraw from these principles when faced with the requirements of a pre-set curriculum and the rigid demands of testing. So what can a teacher or school do that fosters true, deep learning and still meets "requirements?" As Yul Brynner, playing the King of Siam, said: *Is puzzlement*. But there's hope for solutions and we present several constructivist strategies and activities below that have the potential of expanded, active, and deep learning. The activities are from *Write for Mathematics* (2007, Rothstein, Rothstein, and Lauber), *English Grammar Instruction That Works* (2009, (Rothstein & Rothstein), and *Writing As Learning* (2007, Rothstein, Rothstein, & Lauber) and are illustrated in Figures 3.6 to 3.18.

CHAPTER THREE STUDENT – CENTERED TEACHING AND LEARNING

Learning is a Search for Meaning

Figures 3.6, 3.7, and 3.8, taken from *Write for Mathematics (2007)*, illustrate imaginary dialogues between an *Earthling* and a *Martian*. Not having lived on Earth, the Martian wants to understand the meaning of **Expanded Notation,** the meaning of the words **Array, Equation**, and *Number Sentence*, and the meaning of *Algebra.* The Martian searches for these meanings in a dialogue with an "expert" Earthling. By creating dialogue situations, your students develop both a sense of curiosity and a means for satisfying that curiosity in a lively give-and-take situation.

Figure 3.6 Dialogue Between a Martian and an Earthling on Expanded Notation

---

The Martian wants the Earthling to answer this question: *"What is expanded notation?"* Following is a possible response focusing on the term-expanded notation.

Martian: I have looked at a lot of mathematics books in your schools and see the term-expanded notation. What does that mean?

Earthling: First, I will give you an example of a whole number: 345. This is a number that appears to be merely three digits—3, 4, and 5. However, on Earth mathematicians figured out that the words we use to express that number—three hundred, forty, five—means that there are 3 hundreds, which we write as 300; there are 4 tens or 4 times 10, which we write as 40; and there are 5 ones.

Martian: That seems complicated to me.

Earthling: I'll show it to you in a simple way. Think of the words we say for 345: *three hundred-- forty-- five.*

In expanded notation (or the long way), we write those words in numbers, using a plus sign: 300 + 40 + 5.

Martian: Now I get it. It's like adding

    300
  + 40
  + 5

That comes to 345.

> **Earthling:** Good. Now show me how you would write the following numbers in expanded notation:
>
> 633
>
> 4204
>
> 30,602
>
> 450,641
>
> 8,392,901
>
> **Martian:** That's easy now. Here they are:
>
> 600 + 30 + 3
>
> 4000 + 200 + 4
>
> 30,000 + 600 + 2
>
> 400,000 + 50,000 + 600 + 40 + 1
>
> 8,000,000 + 300,000 + 90,000 + 2,000 + 900 + 1
>
> **Earthling:** You're a fast learner.
>
> **Martian:** Thanks. But I sure am glad that there is a short cut to expanded notation because it's too tiring to write out all these numbers.

Figure 3.7 Dialogue Between a Martian and an Earthling on the Terms Array, Equation, and Number Sentence

The Martian has heard the words *array, equation*, and *number sentence*.

The Martian asks the Earthling, "What do you mean by the words *array, equation*, and *number sentence* on Earth?"

Following is a possible dialogue on these terms:

Martian: What do you mean by the words *array, equation*, and *number sentence*?

Earthling: An array is a type of arrangement that shows items (objects) or numbers, as in this array of telephones:

If we divide the number of cell phones by two, we get two equal arrays. There are twelve telephones in the total array. By dividing the total array into two arrays, we have six telephones in each array. We can now write an equation to express the division of the array:

12 (telephones) ÷ 2 (arrays) = 6 (telephones in each array). This equation can be simplified as a number sentence to look this way: $12 \div 2 = 6$.

Martian: I think I now understand. But could you give me a definition of *equation*?

Earthling: Of course. An equation is a set of numbers or value on the left side of an equal sign that equals the same number or set of numbers or value that are on the right side.

Figure 3.8 – Dialogue Between a Martian and Earthling on What is Algebra?

The Martian is visiting the algebra class and asks, "What is algebra?" A friendly Earthling gives the Martian this explanation:

Earthling: First, you have to think of algebra as a branch or form of mathematics. Algebra explains the relationships among different values.

Martian: Please give me an example of what you mean.

Earthling: Well, let's talk about what *equals* means. The = sign is important to understanding arithmetic. It means that what is on one side of the = sign has the same value as what is on the other side. For example, if I say 1 + 5 = 2 + ?, you would have to find what makes the value of the left side the same as the value on the right side.

Martian: What makes algebra different from arithmetic?

Earthling: In algebra, we can substitute a letter for a number, but we still have to know that = means that the values on both sides are the same. For example, in algebra, we can say that 8 + 1 = 3x (when a letter is placed next to a number, it means we multiply them together). Whatever we say "x" is worth has to make both sides of the = sign the same value.

Martian: So this is like saying 3 times "what" equals 9.

Earthling: Great.

Martian: But how do I get the answer?

Earthling: Well, there are a couple of ways to go about it, but in algebra, we try to get the letter to stand by itself on one side of the = sign. We call that isolating the letter, in this case, x.

Martian: Show me what you mean.

Earthling: OK. When we do this, don't forget what the = sign means. We start with 8 + 1 = 3x. What do you think we mean when we say we want to isolate the x?

Martian: To get the x by itself.

Earthling: Good. If we are going to keep both sides of the = sign the same value, we have to treat both sides of the = sign the same way. Otherwise, the two sides won't have the same value. If I want 3x to become just x, I have to divide it by 3. Since I am dividing one side of the = sign by 3, I have to divide the other side by 3, too. It looks like this:

      8 + 1 = 3x   9=3x   9 = 3 times x   3=x or x=3

What has happened?

Martian: If we divide both sides by 3 as shown in the equation, the 9 changes to a 3 and the x is isolated. Yea! So now does x = 3?

Earthling: That's it. Both sides of the = sign still have the same value.

Meaning Requires Understanding *Wholes* As Well As Parts

Imagine defining a *cup* as "something that has a handle," or defining a *country* as place where people live, or describing a *dog* as an animal that barks. Yet many of our textbooks limit definitions to the parts instead of the whole. One of the most notorious subjects for limiting definitions to "parts" is grammar which tells us that "noun is a person, place, or thing," a "verb is a word of action" and an "adjective describes a noun."

Other grammar book statements tell us that "A sentence is a complete thought." "The predicate tells the action." And we are warned to never write "fragments or run-ons." In fact, almost all school grammar books focus on the "part" with minimal explanation of the "whole." Because the Latinate grammar we use to describe English is an imposed structure and not the natural explanation of how English works, we struggle with the rules and *exceptions* that arise from the brute force of the word-by-word grammar model. The English language is a language that operates with groups of words providing the meaning in context and these groups of words fall into four simple patterns that students can easily identify through a model called the Exact *Word* http://www.exactword.com/ (retrieved December 1, 2010)

This model (of *Wholes*) represents a shift for us in understanding the whole of the English language from its parts, but not simply *word parts* but *word patterns*. And yet, in English classrooms we continue to see traditional grammar taught as though the definitions of "parts of speech" are so simple. Why bother to teach them? Unfortunately, traditional *Latin* grammar still represents a predominant area of study in schools today and many tests are based on the Latinate model. However, by substituting traditional grammar instruction with the Exact *Word* strategies, based on *English grammar*, students understand the terminology and can construct meanings easily and accurately.

Figures 3.9, 3.10, and 3.11, taken from *English Grammar Instruction That Works* (2009, Rothstein & Rothstein), illustrate the differences in whole vs. part and are based on the relationship of Syntax (putting words together) and Semantics (getting meaning from the word groupings). We hope our illustrations will lead you to check out explanations in other subjects and how they either limit or expand construction of learning and acquisition of knowledge.

Figure 3.9 - The Varieties of Communicating From One Word to Many - This activity gives you a special kind of word arrangement called The Elliptical Sentence. Write what you think might have prompted these elliptical statements. The first one is done for you. Compare your responses with a partner.

Elliptical Sentences	**Possible Statements That Might Have Preceded the Ellipsis**
Tomorrow. (example)	When is the test?
Yes.	
No thanks.	
Maybe.	
Rarely.	
Never.	
Once in a while.	
If you say so.	
Serves you right.	
So what?	
How?	
Where?	
Why?	
Who?	
When?	
How many?	

Figure 3.10 – Seeing the Big Picture Through Morphology

Read the directions. Then complete the grid based on the patterns of the verbs. Finally complete your observations.

Directions: The verb in the English language always has four forms. However, there are some English verbs that have a fifth form. Verbs with five forms always come from the Anglo-Saxon heritage of the English language. Now you know something about the etymology (word history) of these verbs. Follow these steps to complete this template:

• Look at how the verbs' morphs are named: base, verb-s, -ing, past, -en past

• Complete each form. The four forms for the verb *run* have been done and the five forms for the verb *hide* have been done.

• When you have finished your template, work with a classmate. Complete the statement that follows to explain the patterns of these verbs.

• You are on your way to becoming a great *etymological* explainer of the English language.

BASE	VERB-S	-ING	PAST	-en PAST
run	runs	running	ran	not applicable
hide	hides	hiding	hid	hidden
give				
take				
eat				
speak				
buy				
think				
teach				
hit				
quit				

> Complete this statement of your observations. You can work with a partner.
>
> • From this template of the forms of the English verbs, I have made the following observations:
>
> • First, I observed that all of these verbs have at least _____ forms or morphs.
>
> • But then I noticed that some of these verbs also have _____.
>
> • I realized that the verb forms or morphs of the English language are 1 _____, 2 _____, 3 _____, 4 _____, with some verbs having _____.
>
> • When I looked in the first column labeled *past,* I noticed that some verbs _____, while other verbs _____,
>
> • From this template, I now know that all verbs _____

Figure 3.11 Building a Noun Department Story

> Once you realize that a noun is a word that names many categories and you begin to organize the categories, you can build a *Noun Department Store* and create for yourself a huge vocabulary. (You can later build a *Verb Department Store* too). Here's how you and your classmates can get started.
>
> Directions: Set up a "Noun Department Store" with your teacher's help.
>
> • Make the templates below in your notebook by having two pages facing each other. This arrangement is called a double-page spread.
>
> • Fold each of the pages into four columns so you now have eight columns.
>
> • Place these nouns so that they are in the column that names their "category," as shown in the template: *friend, Mexico, cup, zebra, joy, Zeus, truth.*
>
> • Now work with a classmate and add three or more other nouns to each column that fit the category. You can find nouns for these categories on the walls of your classroom or in your textbooks or reading books.
>
> • If you are not sure of a category of a word, place it in the column called "other."
>
> • Then sort the words into their appropriate columns.

Now write a story, an article, or a letter using as many of these nouns as you can to create a brilliant piece of written text!

Person	Place or Location	Object	Animal	Emotion	Deity	Principle	Other
friend	Mexico	cup	zebra	joy	Zeus	truth	discussion
Betty	home	desk	fox	sadness	Hera	honesty	birthday
teacher	street	sink	insect	anger	Apollo	commitment	mathematics
dad	sky	phones	puppy	delight	Mars	virtue	song
babies	rooms	shelf	mammals	love	Isis	sincerity	joke

Now build a Noun Department Story with Noun Affixes, adding your own nouns to this template.

-ion	-ment	-ence/ance	-ness	-ity	-ism
ambition	advancement	attendance	eagerness	creativity	humanism
devotion	bereavement	brilliance	gentleness	curiosity	Hinduism
emotion	commencement	conference	hardness	integrity	naturalism
generation	department	deliverance	neediness	nobility	populism

Learning Expands When Students Make Connections Between Facts and Concepts

Concept - general idea inferred or derived from specific instances

Being able to formulate a concept is being able to see the wholeness from its parts. Students who develop this ability see both the big picture and the parts or pieces that make up that picture. They develop the ability to generalize from details as well as put the details into a framework. In Figure 3.12, the students are given a general statement or *concept*:

Many cities develop along rivers or other waterways.

They are then presented with a Taxonomy of these cities and are asked "What are at least *three reasons* that this appears to be true? First, have an open-ended discussion about why this relationship of river to city has occurred. Have the students enter the reasons in their notebook. Then have each student or students in pairs research a city of personal choice and collect information about the river that it is situated on. We have provided a Profile for writing a statement that shows the connections between rivers and cities.

They are then presented with a Taxonomy of these cities and are asked "What are at least *three reasons* that this appears to be true? First, have an open-ended discussion about why this relationship of river to city has occurred. Have the students enter the reasons in their notebook. Then have each student or students in pairs research a city of personal choice and collect information about the river that it is situated on. We have provided a Profile for writing a statement that shows the connections between rivers and cities.

Figure 3.12 – Cities and Their Rivers

Many of the world's great cities develop along rivers or other waterways. Below is a Taxonomy of these cities and rivers. Select one of these "pairs" and research both the city and the river from information on the Internet or other sources. Then use the Profile following the Taxonomy to write a *Three Reasons Why* statement explaining this relationship of city to river. When you have finished, you can create a brochure about your city and its river, with an invitation to take a boat ride and see the city's sites. (You can add other cities and rivers).

	CITY	COUNTRY	RIVER
A	Alexandria	Egypt	Nile
B	Baghdad	Iraq	Tigris
C	Calcutta	India	Hugli
D	Damascus	Syria	Barada
	Detroit	United States	Detroit
E			
F			
G	Gabarone	Botswana	Limpopo
H	Ho Chi Minh City	Vietnam	Saigon
I	Istanbul	Turkey	Bosphorus (River)
J	Jakarta	Indonesia	Liwung
K	Kiev	Ukraine	Dnieper
L	Lisbon	Portugal	Tagus
	London	England	Thames
	Lima	Peru	Rimac
	Livingstone	Zambia	Zambesi
M	Madrid	Spain	Manzanares
	Minneapolis	United States	Mississippi

	Montreal	Canada	St. Lawrence
	Melbourne	Australia	Yarra
	Moscow	Russia	Moskva
N	New York	United States	Hudson
	New Orleans	United States	Mississippi
O			
P	Paris	France	Seine
	Pittsburgh	United States	Susquehanna/Monongahela
Q			
R	Rome	Italy	Tiber
	Rio de Janeiro	Brazil	Guandu
S	Shanghai	China	Yangtze
T	Teheran	Iran	Karuj & Jarud
U			
V	Vienna	Austria	Danube
W	Warsaw	Poland	Vistula
X			
Y			
Z	Zagreb	Croatia	Sava
	Zurich	Switzerland	Limmat

Now start your research by checking out one of the cities above or a city you have added, Find a map that locates the city on its river. Then complete the Profile, followed by a brochure that offers people a boat ride on this river. The boat ride should tell the sights you would see and the importance of the river to the city.

THE CITY OF _____ AND ITS RIVER NAMED THE _____

I recently took a job as a travel guide for the city of _____ in _____. One of my tasks as a guide is to tell visitors about the river, which is called _____, and why it is important to the life of the city.

There are at least three reasons why the city of _____ was built along the banks of the _____ river.

First, _____

In addition, _____

Finally, _____

When you take a boat ride along the _____ River, you will discover many important sites. Here are three sites that you should not miss.

First, there is _____

After that, you must see _____

Above all, don't forget _____

After you have taken the tour, I will be available to answer your questions. Please write three questions about the city and the river that you would like me to answer.

 1) _____
 2) _____
 3) _____

Thank you for traveling with me along the _____ and the exciting and interesting city of _____.

Analyzing, Comparing, and Predicting Foster High-Level Learning

Many teachers have assigned students to write a "comparison" essay, comparing, for example, two authors or two characters, or comparing two cities, or possibly comparing a triangle with a rectangle. For many students, this genre of comparing is highly challenging unless there has been direct *instruction* on the structure of comparing. Some teachers use the Venn Diagram, others use David Hyerle's Double Bubble (1995), and sometimes the teacher simply has the students write out two charts.

Once again, we would like to propose the strategy of Defining Format (2007 Rothstein, Rothstein, & Lauber) which uses a template that first allows the students to *categorize* the term (or topic) they are writing about (ex. a planet is a *body in space*) which then allows for *analyzing* or setting out its *characteristics* (ex. orbits around the sun, etc.). Once this information has been gathered, the student can compare a planet with another body in space such as a moon or star or asteroid. By combining the category with the characteristics, the students have an open sentence for developing a comparative essay that can lead to further comparisons and predictive possibilities, as in the example below:

A planet is a body in space that:
1. Orbits around the sun
2. Is made of gases and other related matter
3. May rotate on its axis
4. May have moons or rings (add more)

The students now write a Defining Format for *"What is a moon?"* with a similar analysis and can compare a planet with a moon. Finally, they can speculate or *predict* with a set of open-ended questions.

1. Why don't all planets have moons?
2. What are the possibilities for planets without moons to eventually have moons?
3. What do you think is the likelihood that other stars (suns) have planets and that these planets have moons?

Cite evidence for your speculations or predictions.

Defining Format is a powerful, yet simple, construct that can be introduced as early as first grade and can be used in every subject. The teaching aspect of this strategy is guiding or directing the students toward stating the category rather than using the word *something*. For example, in response to the question, "What is a jacket?" a student might answer, "A jacket is a type of clothing" (not "something you wear"). By helping students to state the category, the teacher shows them how items can be classified or categorized. An excellent way to begin Defining Format is to have the students create a Taxonomy of words related to a category that you might be teaching (e.g. types of clothing).

Figure 3.13 Definition of a Colony – After you have read this definition and discussed the questions that follow, make a list of other political divisions (example: country, state, city) using Defining Format to list the characteristics. Then you can compare and analyze the differences among political divisions.

QUESTION	CATEGORY	CHARACTERISTICS
What is a colony? A colony is a	type of political division that	1) results when a more powerful political division, such as an empire or nation creates, or dominates it 2) is under the control of the dominating nation as to its governance, economy, rights of the indigenous population, trade, and other aspects of life 3) is created for the benefit of the dominating political division (empire, country) 4) "belongs to" or is owned by the dominating power

Once the students have defined the term "colony", they can apply the definition to expand their knowledge and analysis with questions such as:

- Who were the dominating empires that colonized the American continents?
- How were the indigenous (native) peoples affected by the colonization?
- How were the settlers of the colony affected by the role and rule of the colonizers?
- What problems resulted for the "colonists"?
- What solutions did the colonizers use or try to maintain their control of the colonists?
- What are the benefits of colonization to the colonizers?
- What problems and difficulties do colonists face under the rule of their colonizers?
- Why are colonists likely to rebel against their colonizers?

Using Literature for Analyzing, Comparing, and Predicting

From the early grades on, students are likely to read fables which are often just simply defined as a story that teaches a lesson. Well many stories teach a lesson, but they are not all fables. So Defining Format, Figure 3.14, will set out the definition.

Figure 3.14 – Definition of a Fable - You probably have read some fables, especially those by Aesop. Here is an expanded definition to help you tell what a fable is to a friend or family member. You also can now compare a fable with a folk tale or myth or legend by completing Defining Formats about these different "genres".

Question	Category	Characteristics
What is a fable? A fable is a	story genre that	1) tells a moral or teaches a lesson 2) usually, but not always, uses animals as the major characters, a style known as *anthropomorphic* usage 3) is short and to the point 4) has been made famous by the Greek writer Aesop and the French writer LaFontaine, among others. 5) is found in many cultures 6) has become known through generational retellings

Here are three more Defining Formats for the story genres of legend, myth, and folk tale in Figures 3.15, 3.16, and 3.17.

Figure 3.15 -- Definition of a Legend

Question	Category	Characteristics
What is a legend? A legend is a	story genre that	1) begins with a germ of historic truth 2) usually has a male hero: David from David & Goliath (Bible); King Arthur, Robin Hood (British), Manco Capac (Inca) 3) usually pits the good hero against an evil opponent 4) is part of all cultures: Greek, American Indian, Chinese, Persian, African, and more 5) has become known through generational retellings

Figure 3.16 – Definition of a Folk Tale

Question	Category	Characteristics
What is a folk tale? A folk tale is a	story genre that	1) usually has exaggeration of events 2) usually has a male hero from "plain folk"—Davy Crockett, Paul Bunyan 3) may be based on a historic person 4) may have an anthropomorphic hero as in Anansi the Spider 5) is part of all cultures: Greek, American Indian, Chinese, African, Turkish, and more 6) has become known through generational retellings

Figure 3.17 – Definition of a Myth

Question	Category	Characteristics
What is a myth? A myth is a	story genre that	1) explains a scientific idea or natural occurrence in a non-scientific way 2) is based on Why? and How? questions, such as "Why are there stars in the sky?" or "How did humans get fire?" 3) frequently uses gods and goddesses, but may also have animals, real and imaginary 4) may have an exaggeration of events 5) is part of all cultures: Greek, American Indian, Chinese, African, Japanese, and more 6) has become known through generational retellings

A clear and simple way to offer the students a simplified categorization system is illustrated in Figure 3.18, followed by a Frame that helps them write an analysis and comparison of these story genres.

Here is a outline for comparing the four literary genres that you have defined. Next to the Characteristic, write the names of the genres that illustrate this characteristic. There is one example to get you started.

When you have finished, complete the Frame.

Figure 3.18 - MAJOR CHARACTERISTICS OF FOUR LITERARY GENRES: FABLE, LEGEND, FOLK TALE, and MYTH

> Here is a Framed Outline for comparing the four literary genres that you have defined.
>
> You can expand your ideas in this Frame by adding examples and details.
>
> We have been reading four different literary genres: _____, _____, _____, and _____.
>
> Here are examples of specific names of these story genres:
>
> _____, _____, _____, and
>
> _____.
>
> These story genres have both similarities and differences. For example, _____
> _____.
>
> I also noticed _____
> _____,
>
> Furthermore, I realized _____
> _____.
>
> By reading these genres and comparing them, I now know _____
> _____.

We also suggest that you post a model template of a Defining Format and continue to emphasize "writing to a Martian"—someone who is not likely to know what these terms mean. As students learn more about the topic or item, they add this information to the

Defining Format template so that there is an ongoing note-taking system. When the students have completed their Defining Format(s), they can write a Metacognition Statement using the information they have gathered:

A simple starter can be, "As a result of writing a Defining Format about a dog, I know five important facts that I would tell to a Martian."
At a higher level of writing, a student could add, "While all these facts or characteristics fit a dog, the most important characteristic is that it can be domesticated, which means. . "
A more advanced level of writing might include the sentence, "Dogs are a member of the canine family and trace their lineage to the wolves."

FINDING YOUR *NICHE*, BUILDING YOUR INTERESTS
(From Middle French (MF), from nicher which means to make a nest)

Constructive principles also address learning as an individual process as well as a group or social process. Our own slogan is "Everyone knows something that someone else doesn't know" and it is this statement that permits all of us to learn from each other. In addition, this individualized self-knowledge, when tapped into in the classroom, can be the most enriching part of group learning. The concept of each individual's personal knowledge leads to the constructivist principles that state:

> **The purpose of learning is to construct meaning, not just memorize the "right" answer or state someone else's meaning.**

With this principle accepted and posted in the classroom, we can begin the school year with each student from the primary grades through high school, making or writing a Metacognition Statement (Rothstein, Rothstein & Lauber 2007) and sharing it with classmates. (See Figure 3.19.)

From these Metacognition statements, you can now build a Taxonomy, visibly posted in the classroom and frequently revised as students acquire more knowledge as illustrated in Figure 3.19. (More than one name maybe next to a topic)

Figure 3.19 – We Know That We Know Something About…..

	TOPIC	MY NAME
A		
B		
C	cars	Joanna
D		
E		
F		
G		
H		
I	ice cream	La Verne
J		
K		
L		
M		
N		
O		
P	planets	Mitchell
Q		
R	reptiles	Jimmy
S		
T		
U		
V		
W		
X		
Y		
Z		

Now write a Metacognition statement for posting in your classroom so that you can share your knowledge with classmates who would like to know what you know.

I know that I know something about _____

First, I know _____

In addition, I also know _____

Finally, I know _____

You can also add to this note:

If you would like to know something about what I know, you can just ask during free time or text me, or twitter me, or ask the teacher permission for us to chat in the classroom.

You will notice that the information the student provides can be both generic and well-known as well as personalized. All aspects of knowledge are then shared and can be expanded and researched. By encouraging and acknowledging your students' knowledge, you help them develop their own *niche* for learning and allow them to build a powerhouse of interests. From these Metacognition statements, you have the potential for relating the "required" curriculum to students' interests and making each student an "expert" in a field of knowledge.

Let's Have a Date

Teachers have often debated whether "memorizing dates" is necessary for understanding or remembering history. Yet without knowing key dates, we are unable to place historic or memorable events into a context. If we don't connect 1776 with the 4th of July or Independence Day, we are missing the one of the most significant aspects of American history. In the United States, dates such as 1607, 1609, 1619 and later on 1787, 1803, 1835, 1845, and further on, 1865, 1898, 1914, 1917, 1941, 1945 and so forth, anchor our knowledge of history and historic events, and give us each our *niche* for deeper understanding.

So we would like to suggest that, beginning in the intermediate grades, classrooms have Chronology Walls, much like word walls with significant words, and that every student selects a year of importance and becomes the class expert on that year. Once again, the Internet can be a great contributor along with books, parents, teachers, and friends, among other possibilities.

Below is a chronology of the years 490 BCE to 1621 that Evelyn (one of the authors) remembers from her school years in the Bronx, from P.S. 70, JHS 117, and William Howard Taft High School. (She remembers later years too!) Following this chart is Figure 3.20 for students to create their own chronology.

EVELYN'S CHRONOLOGY OF HISTORIC DATES FROM 490 BCE TO 1621 CE

490 BCE – Battle of Marathon in Ancient Greece, resulting in Marathons of today

325 CE – Constantine – First Christian Roman Emperor

476 CE – Fall of Rome according to Edwin Gibbons, Historian

1066 – William of Normandy crosses English Channel and defeats King Harold at Battle Of Hastings

1215 – Writing of the Magna Carta, at Runnymede, England

1278 – Marco Polo meets Kubla Khan

1453 – Ottoman Empire at the Gates of Vienna

1497 – Americus Vespucci sails to South America, giving America its name

1564 – Birth of William Shakespeare, April 23, in Stratford-upon-Avon

1607 – Settlement of Jamestown

1609 – Arrival of Henry Hudson in (what would later be) New York

1619 – First slaves arrive in Virginia, women settlers arrive in Virginia, House of Burgesses established in Virginia

1620 – Arrival of Pilgrims at Plymouth Rock

1621- Pilgrims and the Wampanoag celebrate first Thanksgiving

Figure 3.20 – Creating Your Own Chronology –

Chronos was a Greek mythological figure who was the keeper of time and today the word "chronology" means both the keeping of and the study of time. Create your personal chronology by researching major or significant world events that happened during the year you were born up to the present time of your age. For example, if you are twelve years old, you would find twelve events from around the world. The events can be from sports, politics, births or deaths of famous people, different countries or the United States, or from any other subject that you find interesting. SHARE your chronology with family and friends. Here's a model you can use. Place the year and the event in each box in chronological order. You can use sticky paper or poster paper or other forms and enter the year and event. You can also add a paragraph or more about the importance of each event.

I was born in the year _____, so I am now _____ years old. During these years, the following significant events took place around the world.

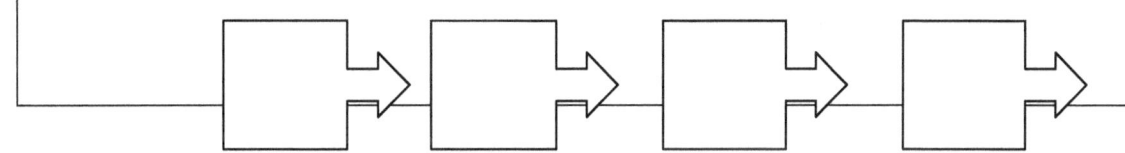

CHAPTER 4

Individualizing Curriculum & Instruction Matched to the Needs, Talents, and Interests of ALL Learners

> **standard**
> 1. a rule or principle considered by an authority or by general consent as a basis of comparison; an approved model.
> 2. a rule or principle that is used as a basis for judgment: *They tried to establish standards for a new philosophical approach.*
> 4. an average or normal requirement, quality, quantity, level, grade, etc.: *His work this week hasn't been up to his usual standard.*
> 5. standards, those morals, ethics, habits, etc., established by authority, custom, or an individual as acceptable:

"All states and schools will have challenging and clear standards of achievement and accountability for all children, and effective strategies for reaching those standards." -- U.S. Dept. of Education

Common Core State Standards Initiative

> **"All states and schools will have challenging and clear standards of achievement and accountability for all children, and effective strategies for reaching those standards." -- U.S. Dept. of Education**
>
> **Common Core State Standards Initiative**
> "The Common Core State Standards Initiative is a state-led effort coordinated by the National Governors Association Center for Best Practices (NGA Center) and the Council of Chief State School Officers (CCSSO)....These standards define the knowledge and skills students should have within their K-12 education careers so that they will graduate high school able to succeed in entry-level, credit-bearing academic college courses and in workforce training programs. The standards:
>
> - Are aligned with college and work expectations;
> - Are clear, understandable and consistent;
> - Include rigorous content and application of knowledge through high-order skills;
> - Build upon strengths and lessons of current state standards;
> - Are informed by other top performing countries, so that all students are prepared to succeed in our global environment

All schools (in the United States) are expected to be "standards-based." This seems like a sensible idea, especially if we were to take the opposite position and say that schools do not have to have standards. The problem we see with (worthwhile) standards is often the failure to mention or recognize that every human being has "strengths" in some or even many areas, but can still lack "strengths" in other areas. Mathematically gifted students may or may not be gifted in poetry. The students who are "computer whizzes" may or may not be top spellers or be capable of remembering the dates of the explorations or knowing how to draft a persuasive essay. In fact, it is this amazing diversity of abilities and capabilities that allow some of us to be artists and others to be scientists, some to be great cooks, and others to be great baseball pitchers or soccer players

.

What is a school to do?

In Chapter 3 we wrote of knowing what your students know and making this knowledge the centrality of your school or classroom. With this knowledge, we can add the mantra of Feuerstein from his seminal work *Instrumental Enrichment* (2006) which states over and over again "Intelligence is modifiable" as long as we believe that every human has the capacity to learn and that those of us who teach are the mediators of that learning. We have selected one of the standards from above—the one we believe transcends all the others—and will make it the "standard bearer" for the whole school. It is stated below with one modification. Instead of "include" which gives an underlying option to not include, we have substituted "**insist on**" and have added **thinking and inquiry and for all students and mediated by every teacher.**

Therefore,

Insist on rigorous content and application of knowledge through high-order thinking and inquiry skills for all students, which is intentionally *mediated* **to every student by every teacher.**

Mediation, through the action of a mediator, implies deliberation that results in solutions. With this concept, we offer ideas and strategies that recognize the individual students' strengths and interests and provide activities that can capitalize on these strengths, while still maintaining the models of social and constructivist learning that we wrote about in Chapter 3.

We start with the standard that asks us be to "informed by other top performing countries, so that all students are prepared to succeed in our global economy and society; and are evidence-based." We see this standard to be in full alignment with a culturally responsive school and which can serve as our beacon for "Defining Excellence."

Currently, Finland has the distinction of being one of the top-performing educational systems and has become a model for countries around the world. We have drawn our information from Finnish Ministry of Education and Culture and cite three areas in Figure 4.1 where Finland has developed unique and wide-reaching programs that are both "individualized" and generic, so that all students can benefit from their special interests as well as school and cultural expectations. This is followed by Figure 4.2 which is a joint survey of the OECD member countries (Organization for Economic Co-operation and Development), and a number of other countries and PISA (Program for International Student Assessment). .

Figure 4.1 Three Citations from the Finnish Educational System

State prize for translation to Hebrew translator Rami Saari

(26.8.) This year's state prize for translation has been awarded to Rami Saari, in recognition of his distinguished and wide-ranging work transmitting Finnish literature to Hebrew-speaking readers. The monetary prize (10,000 Euros) is a substantial one in international terms, and is a tribute to a translator's important but often unheralded work. The prize is awarded annually by the Finnish Ministry of Education and Culture based on the recommendation of FILI – Finnish Literature Exchange.

Committee proposes extra hours and a greater range of elective studies in basic education

(26.8.) A committee has been deliberating on the national objectives for basic education and reforms to the distribution of lesson hours.

It proposes that more elective subjects be included in basic education and that ethics and drama be introduced as new subjects. The committee also proposes that the number of lesson hours in arts and physical education be increased. The proposal of the committee is circulated for comments, on the basis of which a government decree will be drafted to be issued in early 2011.

Excellent PISA-results for Finnish students

The knowledge and skills of Finnish students in science, mathematics and reading are of the highest order. In science and mathematics they are rated best in the OECD countries and in reading the second best. The main focus in PISA 2006 was science literacy.

"We are delighted that our deliberate and continued investment in education has again been rewarded with the top position in the Pisa ranking", said Minister of Education. "In a global economy education is key to Finland retaining its competitive edge. We will continue to focus on equipping our students to participate fully in society both in and beyond school."

Figure 4.2 Survey of Organization for Economic Co-operation and Development, and Student Assesment

The tests are administered in schools every three years to 15-year-olds in the domains of mathematics, science, reading literacy and problem-solving skills. The main focus of the first (PISA 2000) was reading and in the second (PISA 2003) mathematics, while this latest, PISA 2006, focused on science.

The survey will assess how 15-year-olds master the essential knowledge and skills necessary for work and the quality of life in future society. The survey will not directly assess how well students master the actual contents of the curricula.

Finland's success in the PISA survey

The skills of Finnish students were among the best in all domains assessed in PISA surveys (2000, 2003,2006).

- In reading literacy: first place in two surveys (2000,2003) and second place (2006)
- In mathematics, Finnish students were fourth (2000) and second (2003) and first (2006)
- In science, they were third (2000), joint first (2003) and first (2006)
- In problem-solving skills, they were joint second (2003, not assessed in 2000)
- Finland's score (2006) is the best result ever achieved in any subject area in any of the PISA surveys

The uniformity of students' performance is a special forte in Finland. The differences between the strongest and weakest results in Finland are among the smallest in the survey. Differences between schools and regions are also remarkably small in Finland. Differences in performance were very slight between various language groups in Finland, and the socio-economic background has a lower impact on students' performance here than in the other PISA countries. A significant implication is that high performance can be achieved with relatively low differences in performance between students.

Before we move on, we want to emphasize that comparing educational performances among different countries or cultures can lead to false conclusions. Differences related to diversity, economics, value systems, and other factors do or can contribute to school achievement so that comparisons can be misleading. However, we strongly believe that focusing on engaging, interactive, high level instruction works everywhere. And with this ardent belief system, we continue with classroom strategies and activities that define excellence and result in student success.

The uniformity of students' performance is a special forte in Finland. The differences between the strongest and weakest results in Finland are among the smallest in the survey. Differences between schools and regions are also remarkably small in Finland. Differences in performance were very slight between various language groups in Finland, and the socio-economic background has a lower impact on students' performance here compared to other PISA countries. A significant implication is that high performance can be achieved with relatively low differences in performance between students.

We believe that high performance is possible for students coming from different languages and different socio-economic groups when we focus on students' needs, talents and qualities, and interests. Using our Taxonomy system, we have made three start-up lists as a model for this concept and we strongly suggest that you develop this Taxonomy with *input from your own students,* keep it posted, and add to it as it changes. Figure 4.3 illustrates this Taxonomy.

Figure 4.3 Sample Taxonomy of Students' Needs, Talents and Qualities, and Interests (Talents and Interests May Overlap)

	NEEDS	TALENTS & QUALITIES	INTERESTS
A	attention	artistry, ambition, accurateness	art, animals
B	belief in potential	broad-mindedness	bicycling, baseball, basketball, boating
C	caring	conscientiousness, curiosity	chess, cooking, computer games, cats
D	depth	dramatic flair, determination	drama, dance, double-dutch, dogs, drums, dinosaurs
E	equality	empathy	
F	friendship	friendliness, fair-mindedness	fishing
G	generosity	graciousness	games
H	honesty, humor	humorous, hard-working	hip-hop, horseback riding
I	incentives	industriousness	
J	justice	joyousness	jump-roping, jogging, jokes
K	knowledge	kindness	
L	love	laughter	
M	magnanimity	musicality	math games, movies
N	nobility		
O	open-mindedness	organization	
P	patience	participatory	puzzles, piano playing
Q	quality	quick-minded	
R	reasonableness	rationality	rapping, reading, reptiles
S	sympathy	social-awareness	swimming, storytelling, songwriting, singing
T	truthfulness	tolerance	television, traveling
U	understanding		
V	value, veracity	vision	video games
W	warmth, wisdom	wonderment	water sports
X	excellence	excitement	
Y	youthfulness		
Z	zest	zealousness	

By creating Taxonomy of Needs, Talents, Qualities, and Interests early in the school year, we can begin to relate the curriculum to the students and the students to the curriculum. This inter-relationship can be developed by personalized strategies and activities, many of which can be an integral part of teaching writing, since writing lends itself to self-expression. Figures 4.4 through Figure 4.8 provide you with Frames that your students can use to write about themselves and share with others. Chapter 8, *"Who's Who"* in *Writing As Learning* (2007) is a source for these and other autobiographic and biographic frames that can be incorporated into the concepts of focusing on Needs, Talents, Qualities, and Interests.

WHAT IS A FRAME?

A Frame is another organizing template that provides students with a structure for writing a story, an explanation, or a narrative. It is a textual outline that helps students get started and to focus on the topic through use of transition words or narrative markers. A Frame is useful as an instructional approach to guide students in the early stages of writing, such as sentence and paragraph development. When students use Frames, they begin to internalize the formal structures that writing demands and, over time, move to independent writing while retaining organization and a consistent point of view.

Figure 4.4. Writing About One of Your Interests: Select a sport or game that interests you. Check books, magazines, and the Internet for information on that sport or game. When you have completed the Profile, write a sports article telling a person who is unfamiliar with the sport or game what she or he needs to know to understand it or play it.

Name of Sport or Game _____

Number of Players Required_____

Countries Where Popular _____

Equipment Needed _____

Uniform Items _____

Names of Team Positions (e.g. pitcher, goalie)

_____

_____

_____

Scoring Terms

_____

_____

Other Special Terms

_____

_____

Object or Purpose (e.g. cross finish line first)

_____

_____

Other Information

_____

_____

_____

Figure 4.5 A Frame About Your Teacher and You

My teacher's name is _____

She/He teaches me many subjects and ideas that will help me later in life

First, _____
_____

In addition,
_____
_____

Furthermore,
_____
_____

I believe that by learning what she/is teaching, I will
_____
_____
_____

Figure 4.6. A Personal Profile -- Use this Profile to write information about yourself. When the Profile is completed, write a description of yourself, or use the Profile for information when you write your autobiography.

First Name _____ Middle Name _____

Last Name _____ Other Names _____

ADDRESS (for local and interplanetary use)*

House Number _____

Street (Avenue, Road, Lane, Circle, etc.) _____

Borough, Village, Town, or City _____

State _____ Zip Code _____ Country _____

Continent _____ Hemisphere _____

Planet _____

BIRTH INFORMATION

Date of Birth _____ Place of Birth _____

Present Age _____

PHYSICAL DESCRIPTION

Height _____ Weight _____ Color of Eyes _____ Color of Hair _____

Other physical characteristics (tall, curly hair) _____

PERSONAL INTERESTS

Sports I Enjoy _____

Favorite Television Programs _____
_____

Movies I've Enjoyed _____
_____

Music I Play and/or Music I Like _____

SCHOOL INFORMATION

School I'm Attending _____

Schools I've Attended _____

Best School Subjects _____

After-School Activities _____

Most Memorable Teachers _____

Figure 4.7 My Dream -- Use the Frame to write your dream of the future. You probably have more than one dream, so use this Frame as often as you like to express your ideas. Your dream might be about your personal life or about how you might help others.

I have a dream that _____

In this dream, I see myself _____

To make this dream come true, I _____

_____

_____

Figure 4.8 Sharing Your Knowledge – By having interests, you have much to share with your classmates, friends, and family. Use this frame as an example of what you know. You can change the question to match your interest, but keep the same framework.

How do we know so much about animals that roamed Earth millions of years ago? I would like to answer this question for you.

Most of our knowledge comes from _____

From this knowledge, we learn _____

_____

We also learn _____

Finally, we learn _____

_____

Fossils are found in many places.

They may be _____

_____

Another place to look would be _____

_____

Sometimes fossils are found _____

_____

Fossils are formed in several ways. Sometimes _____

A second way _____

Then there are fossils that _____

By studying fossils, we better understand _____

Humor in the Classroom - A Serious Need

> **humor**
>
> 1. a comic, absurd, or incongruous quality causing amusement: *the humor of a situation.*
> 2. the faculty of perceiving what is amusing or comical: *He is completely without humor.*
> 3. an instance of being or attempting to be comical or amusing; something humorous: *The humor in his joke eluded the audience.*
> 4. the faculty of expressing the amusing or comical: *The author's humor came across better in the book than in the movie.*

In our search for standards, we have not found a standard that states "students shall recognize and create humor in their academic studies". Yet imagine a humorless world without jokes, puns, satire, plays on words, comedy, pantomime, and who knows what else that brings laughter to our lives. Surely every student is "interested in humor."

You may wish to create your own curriculum of humor, but to get you started, we are presenting several activities from Chapter 10 in *English Grammar Instruction That Works* (2009) that relate grammar to word play, or from another viewpoint makes what might be a *boring* subject (grammar) into *fun* (word play). We begin with two quotes in Figure 4.9 from our two favorite humorous books -- *Alice in Wonderland* by Lewis Carroll (1861) and *The Phantom Tollbooth* by Norton Justin (1989).

> *"Mine is a long and sad tale! said the Mouse turning to Alice and sighing. "It is a long tail, certainly, said Alice, looking down with wonder at the Mouse's tail; but why do you call it sad?"* (from *Alice's Adventures in Wonderland*, Carroll, 1861/1995, p.30)
>
> *You have committed the following crimes…sowing confusion, upsetting the applecart, wreaking havoc, and mincing words.* (from the Police Officer Short Shrift in *The Phantom Tollbooth*, Juster, 1989, p. 62)

Figure 4.9 – What's So Funny?

By introducing and including humor into your curriculum, you are not only making your students laugh and have fun (both good), you are also giving them top-of-the -line language instruction that includes, but is not limited to:

- metaphors, similes, and idioms
- oxymora
- eponyms
- colorful words
- affixes (awry)
- comedic characters

Figures 4.10 to Figure 4.15 are examples of word play activities that are among the possible examples for bringing humor into the curriculum.

Figure 4.10 Body Language

Directions: Here are examples of idioms that use body words to give an image of something different from the actual or literal words. For example, "to have eyes in the back of the head" means you know what is going on all around. Select five of these idioms, and write a story using these five idioms in the same story. There is an example following the list. Illustrate your story if you wish.

BONE—cut to the bone, bare bones, bone of contention

EYES—eyes in back of the head

EARS—all ears, bend someone's ear

EYEBROWS—raise one's eyebrows

FACE—face up, do an about face

FINGER–at one's fingertips, have a finger in the pie, cross your fingers

FEET—feet of clay, put one's foot in one's mouth, get one's foot in the door

HEAD—head and shoulders above the crowd, come to a head

HEART—have a warm heart, take heart, heart in my mouth

LIPS—her lips are sealed, button your lips

MOUTH—put your money where your mouth is

MIND—read my mind

MUSCLES—flex your muscles

NECK–stick out one's neck

NOSE—a nose for news

PALM—grease one's palm

SHOULDER—get the cold shoulder, cry on my shoulder

TEETH—grit one's teeth, armed to the teeth, by the skin of my teeth, fight tooth and nail, gnash one's teeth, cut one's teeth

TONGUE—at the tip of my tongue, get a tongue lashing

Example of a Story Using "Body Language"

By knowing idioms you will be *head and shoulders* above the crowd. You will have numerous phrases *at your fingertips* and will be able to get your *foot in the door* for many good jobs. In discussions, you will be able to *cut to the bone* when it comes to ideas and *put your money where your mouth is*. So don't worry about *sticking your neck out* on these words. Just *flex your [linguistic] muscles* and *become all ears* so that you can learn these phrases.

Figure 4.11 Oxymora The oxymoron is a phrase with contradictory words (e.g., *a small fortune*) that comes from two Greek words that are semantically opposite, meaning *sharply dull*. Select six of these oxymora and write a statement explaining why these words say what is "impossible" or contradictory. Examples follow the taxonomy.

A	almost always, almost never, almost impossible
B	big sip, baby grand (piano)
C	calm winds, clever fool
D	down elevator
E	exact estimate
F	false facts, fresh frozen foods
G	good grief
H	half empty, half true
I	ill health, inside out
J	junk food, just war
K	know less
L	lesser evil, loud whisper
M	minor disaster
N	near miss, nearly complete
O	old news, open secret
P	partial silence, perfect idiot
Q	quiet revolution, quiet scream
R	restless sleep, random order, rules of war
S	second best, sad clown
T	terribly good, tense calmness
U	unwelcome recess, unbiased opinion
V	vaguely aware, voluntary taxes
W	whole half, working vacation, wickedly good
X	extreme kindness
Y	young sixty
Z	zero defects

Examples of the Contradiction (Opposites) in Oxymora

Minor disaster—A disaster means a terrible event or tragedy. Minor means small or trivial. So how could a disaster be minor?

Working vacation—When we take a vacation, we don't expect to work. So how could we have a working vacation?

Figure 4.12 Eponyms -- Eponyms are words that come from people's names, such as Boycott and Fahrenheit. By learning eponyms, you get to know about famous (and infamous) people and the inventions or stories related to their names. Figure 4.12 gives a list of famous eponyms. The people listed in this Taxonomy have become famous as words in our language. Sometimes the name has changed its form or the way it is used. For example, the Greek character named Arachne who was an excellent spinner became the word "arachnid" referring to a spider.

Another example is John Montagu, the Fourth Earl of Sandwich in England, who wanted to have more time to gamble and needed a quick way to eat. One day his servant put some meat between two pieces of bread and soon people everywhere were eating "a sandwich." Research the story of three or four of the people in this Taxonomy, and write the story of how their names became eponyms. Then write a statement telling how you might become an eponym yourself by making some contribution to humanity. An example follows the Taxonomy.

EPONYMS TO KNOW

A	Arachne
B	Boycott (Charles), Braille (Louis)
C	Celsius (Anders)
D	Diesel (Rudolph), Doberman (Ludwig)
E	Eiffel (Alexandre Gustave), Echo
F	Fahrenheit (Gabriel Daniel)
G	Guppy (Robert)
H	Hygeia
I	Iris
J	Janus, Juno
K	Kevin (William Thomas)
L	Leotard (Julius)
M	Morpheus, Melba (Nellie)
N	Nicot (Jean)
O	Ohm (George Simon)
P	Pasteur (Louis)
Q	Quixote (Don)
R	Richter (Charles)
S	Silhouette (Etienne de)
T	Titans
U	
V	Volta (Alessandro)
W	Watt (James)
X	
Y	
Z	Zeppelin (Count Ferdinand Von)

Here's another example of becoming an Eponym

> Name of Person—Louis Pasteur
>
> Eponym—pasteurize, pasteurization
>
> Event or Story—Louis Pasteur was a scientist in the 1800s who observed that many people would become very ill from drinking cow's milk. In searching for the cause, he discovered that milk and milk products such as cheese, often contained harmful bacteria although he wasn't sure why they were harmful. He experiment with heating the milk to a temperature that could destroy the bacteria without changing or spoiling the taste. His experiments were successful and to this day we still *pasteurize* milk and milk products.

Be an Eponym - Think of a product or an invention that you might make or that you will develop. Then name that product or invention after your first or last name or use some part of your name. For example, if your name is Andy, you might develop a highly nutritious fruit bar that provides lots of energy and vitamins. Soon people will be calling these bars "Andy's" or "Andy Bars." Use the Frame to guide your writing.

> Your first or last name
> _____
>
> Your invention or contribution to society
> _____
>
> How your name has become "eponized"
> _____

Figure 4.13 Colorful Words and Phrases

The English language uses words of color to express different meanings, such as *true blue*, *gray matter*, and many others. Figure 4.13 gives a list of many of these "colorful phrases." Write your own story using as many of these phrases as you can. Then illustrate each phrase if you wish. An example follows the Taxonomy.

Figure 4.13 COLORFUL PHRASES IN THE ENGLISH LANGUAGE

COLORFUL PHRASE	MEANING
True blue	Loyal
Feeling blue	Down-hearted
Bolt from the blue	An unexpected event
Once in a blue moon	Rarely or seldom
Singing the blues	Feeling or acting sad
Green thumb	Good at gardening
Gray matter	smart brains
Silver lining	inside of a dark cloud telling us that life is better
Black sheep	person who causes shame or embarrassment in a family
In the limelight	Being the center of attention
In the pink	Feeling healthy
In the black	Having enough money
In the red	Owing lots of money
Red-carpet treatment	Being considered honored or important
Red-letter day	Getting good news
Paint the town red	Have a wonderful wild time
Red as a beet	Showing embarrassment
Rose-colored glasses	Seeing the world as good and kind
White elephant	An item that's more expensive than it's worth
White lie	A minor falsehood
Yellow-bellied	A coward
Yellow journalism	News reporting that exaggerates
Write Sentences Using Colorful Expressions	
Here is an example of a "colorful" statement: I have a *true blue* friend who is *as good as gold* and who always gives me the *red-carpet treatment*. Now write several of your own colorful expressions and share them with your classmates. Have fun illustrating these expressions.	

Figure 4.14 Affixes Awry or Missing

Have you ever wondered why we can be *uncouth* but not couth, *ruthless* but not ruthful, *toothless* but not toothful, or *truthf*ul but not truthless? There are numerous words in the English language that can be affixed to have a meaning that is either negative or positive. But often these very words don't "accept" both affixes, as in *helpful* and *helpless* or *happy* and *unhappy*. Interestingly, words that do not seem to have opposite affixes may have started out as opposites (as in *ruthless* and *ruthful*), but over time one survived and the other became obsolete. By studying the etymology of these affixed and "affixless" words, you can gain much information and insight about how vocabulary grows, changes, appears, and disappears.

Directions: The words in this Taxonomy have either a front affix (prefix) or an end affix (suffix). However, we might expect that because of their prefix or suffix, they should also have an opposite affix. For example, we have the word *timeless,* yet we don't have *timeful*. Why not? Work with a partner and select 10 words from this Taxonomy. Then answer the questions beneath each word. Check an unabridged dictionary or the Internet to find out the history (etymology) of the words and why only one form is in use.

A Aimless - What would happen if your behavior was *aimful?*

B Blissful - What would you feel like if you were *blissless?*

C Childless - Describe a family that is *childful.*

D Discombobulated - Describe what you would be doing if you were *combobulated.*

E Eventful - What would be a life that is *eventless?*

F Fretful - Tell what it is like to be *fretless*.

G Grateful - How would someone *grateless* behave?

H Hapless - What is the difference between a hapless person and *a hapful* person?

I Impunity What would be the difference between being treated with impunity compared to being treated with *punity?*

J K

L Listless - How might you change from listless to *listful?*

M Masterful - What would happen to a *masterless* horseback rider?

N Nonchalant - What would be the difference between someone who is *nonchalant* and someone who is *chalant?*

O

P Plentiful - How might one's life go from plentiful to *plentiless?*

Q

R Respectful - What are some characteristics of being *respectless?*

S Sorrowful - What might change a sorrowful mood into a *sorrowless* mood?

T Truthful - How might you treat a person who is *truthless?*

U Unruly - How might we make some unruly students *ruly?*

V Vengeful - What would someone *vengeless* be like?

W Wonderful - What might change a wonderful day into a *wonderless* day?

X

Y Youthful - How might a *youthless* person act youthful?

Z Zestful - Describe a person who is constantly *zestless.*

Comedy in the Classroom

One of the games Evelyn's family would play on rainy days was a game named "Comedic Characters". We would make up characters with names such as *Al Cohol, Ben Evolent, Ella Phant,* and so forth and then do playlets or scenes. Not only was the game fun, but it became a good vocabulary builder. Soon the whole family (four children plus parents) was searching for words that could become characters.

When we introduced Comedic Characters into the classroom, we found that students not only laughed, but they too, like Evelyn's family, went on a search and soon discovered Greg Arious, Cara Smatic, Phil Anthropic, and a host of mainly other Latin and Greek "personalities." Figure 4.15 represents some of the characters. Following the Taxonomy is Figure 4.16, a Character Profile for developing the "character" and other suggestions for building semantic superiority in your students. (Spellings may vary!)

Figure 4.15 Comedic Characters

Directions: These "characters" get their names from words that mostly have Latin and Greek origins. Select one of the characters and complete the character profile that follows. Then meet with three or four of your classmates and share the information you have gathered. After your meeting, write a story with your classmates using your characters.

A	Ann Onymous, Ann Tonym, Al Gebra, Al Gorithm, Ali Mentary
B	Ben Evolent, Ben Efactor, Ben Eficent
C	Cara Smatic, Cal Cium
D	D. Pendent, Dan Dee, Di Agram, Di Aphanous, Di Gest
E	Ella Phant, Evan Escent, Etta Kett
F	Frank O. Phile, Fran Chise
G	Greg Arious
H	Hugh Manity, Hy Gene
I	I. Sosceles
J	Jo Cular
K	Kit Tennish
L	Lu Cent, Leo Tard
M	Mag Nitude, Mel Ifluous, Martin Ett, Moe Bill
N	N. Velop
O	O. Bey
P	Phil Harmonic, Phil Anthropic, Phil Osophy, Phil Ander, Polly Gon
Q	Quint Essence
R	Ray Venn
S	Sue Pine, Stu Pendous, Sal Ubrious, Sal Amander
T	Tim Idd
U	Una Verse, Una Form
V	Val Liant, Vic Torious
W	Wanda Ring
X	Xena Phobic
Y	Yugo Slav
Z	Zig Zag

Figure 4.16 Using Comedic Characters to Create a Character

Here is an example using the comedic character "Wanda Ring" with directions.

• Check the dictionary: Research the word in an unabridged dictionary or on the Internet. Look up the word by base (*wander*, not *wandering*). • Copy the entry or entries as in the following example (e.g., wan·der·ing [wan-der-ing]):

1. moving from place to place without a fixed plan; roaming; rambling: *wandering tourists.*

2. having no permanent residence; nomadic: *a wandering tribe of Indians.*

3. meandering; winding: *a wandering river; a wandering path.*

4. an aimless roving about; leisurely traveling from place to place: *a period of delightful wandering through Italy.*

5. Wanderings: a. aimless travels; meanderings: Her wanderings took her all over the world. b. disordered thoughts or utterances; incoherencies: mental wanderings; the wanderings of delirium; to ramble without a definite purpose or objective; roam, rove, or stray: to wander over the earth.

[bef. 900; ME *wandren,* OE *wandrian* (c. G *wandern*), freq. of *wendan* to WEND; see -ER6] wan er·er, *n.* Syn. 1. range, stroll. 2. saunter. 6. swerve, veer. 8. ramble, rove.

Character Profile: Here is an example of a completed character profile on *Wanda Ring:*

Name of character: Wanda Ring   **Age: 15** (note: when someone might start to wander)

Family background or character: Germanic, Anglo-Saxon; family goes back to the time of Middle English

Habitat: England, United States, and other English-speaking countries

Wishes of character: to see the world; to meander along the rivers and highways; to meet people from everywhere

Fears of character: to be cooped up; to get lost; to be alone

Positive character traits: adventurous, curious, open-minded

Negative or weak character traits: may be aimless, forgetful, inattentive

Paragraph based on previous information: Wanda Ring is an interesting character for many reasons. She is an explorer who always wants to know what is happening in other parts of the world. In addition, she has had a long history in our language, going back to the Anglo-Saxon days. Finally, she is associated with the nomadic peoples of the Earth who travel constantly to find food, water, and better places to live. Wanda Ring has been part of the lives of Bedouins, Berbers, Romas, and many other nomadic peoples in different parts of the world who have always welcomed her into their homes.

CHAPTER 5

SHARED VISION AND COMMITMENT BY ALL STAKEHOLDERS: ADMINISTRATORS, EDUCATORS, PARENTS & CAREGIVERS, STUDENTS, AND ALL SELF-DIRECTED LEARNERS

We all know the role we play in the teaching and learning of those entrusted in our care. As we come to our last chapter, we hope you have a better understanding of what we mean by DEFINING EXCELLENCE in reference to today's learner. To achieve this excellence, we must ALL take responsibility and focus on culturally responsive teaching in every educational setting. The future is NOW. As we become models of DEFINING EXCELLENCE for our self-directed learners, there is that instant when *NOW* becomes *YESTERDAY!* It is our responsibility to be culturally responsive to our learners so that we have the tools and the knowledge to embrace the culture of the 21st century learner.

To provide our students with the knowledge and strategies they need to succeed in this new century requires a continuous "professional development support system" that we define as a network of dedicated educators connecting with each other, implementing, evaluating and re-creating to ensure the gift of quality education. You, the reader, now become part of "WE"—the network of educators always "DEFINING EXCELLENCE". The "WE" is a powerful team, always connected to technology for quality teaching and high-powered learning.

The Continuous Professional Development Model

Stakeholders in quality education must have an understanding that students need to be successful as *self-directed* learners connected to peers. To maintain the optimum level of excellence for best educational practices across disciplines, quality professional development must be an ongoing and integral part of the educational community. In addition, the educational community must be globally connected and constantly in touch with current research and involvement in today's and tomorrow's immersive world to facilitate the connection.

How Teachers Learn

Descriptions of the major models of professional development can be found in the writings of Sparks & Loucks-Horsley (1989). These models include training, observer/assessment, and individually guided models. The training model typically involves a team of presenters considered experts. This traditional professional development model has been around for a long time, with some variations. Workshops, seminars, and conferences are considered the traditional form of training, while reform types of a professional development use study groups, networking, mentoring, coaching, and regular school day meetings that may occur during the process of classroom instruction or planning time (Lee, 2004). These fall in the observer/assessment model type.

The advantages of what Lee refers to as reform types of professional development are that teachers are able to make connections with classroom teaching that are easier to sustain over time. Traditional models of professional development are problematic because they tend to be fragmented, incoherent, and disconnected from the daily work of teachers and students (Hawley & Valli 1999).

Some school districts offer a unified program for all teachers, whereas others leave decisions on the content, format, and timing of developmental activities to the staffs of each school (Seyfarth, 1996). This type of decentralized staff development involves teachers in decisions about program content and format, which lead to higher levels of interest and commitment. Seyfarth also claimed that site-based programs increase collaboration among and between teachers and principals, and that program offerings are more relevant and practical than programs that are centrally directed.

The Challenge

There are several challenges associated with teacher professional development. Between the ringing bells and the standardized class periods, teachers have among the most structured of all careers. Their time for *professional* growth is equally prescribed, often being set by contracts, district policies, and even state law (Sawchuk, 2009). While education has subscribed for decades to a pattern of one and done training, its effectiveness has to be questioned. When looking at the implementation of a new instructional strategy, teachers have traditionally cited inadequate training regarding the strategies and insufficient support in the classroom when they seek to implement these new strategies (Williams & Coles, 2007).

To help teachers incorporate highly effective instructional strategies into their classrooms, countless professional development workshops are offered each year by educational corporations, universities, state governments, and local school systems. Yet, most of these workshops fail to affect true sustainable change in the classroom behavior of teachers (Darling-Hammond, 1995; Sparks & Loucks-Horsley, 1989). One barrier, the research-to-practice gap, is a long-standing issue in education, extensively researched by Bondy and Brownell (2004). Williams & Coles (2007) report that teachers fail to use research information to improve instructional practice because they find it intimidating, are unable to find time to identify needed resources for applying new methods, or have a lack of access to research materials in the first place.

In addition to the research-to-practice gap, teachers' specific barriers to change often block successful implementation of new strategies. For most teachers, it is simply easier and more comfortable to continue with teaching strategies that are tried and true, resulting in an avoidance or fear of new methods (Fullan, 2001). Gess-Newsome, Southerland, Johnston, and Woodbury (2003) described these habits as a "personal practical theory" of teaching in which the teachers' experiences and philosophies dictate an image of how teaching and learning in their classrooms should look (p. 758). Anything contrary to those images has a difficult time taking hold in practice. Finally Johnson (2006) recognized that a school environment perceived as unsafe for change blocks efforts to embrace change, and a lack of administrative support, and the intense focus on accountability through state and national tests results in teachers focusing on "what works" rather than experimenting with new strategies.

Professional Development Goes Online

The U.S. Department of Education released a meta-analysis of online learning studies (Means et al. 2009) that detailed several implications for not only distance learning and web-based learning, but also indicated that much more research is needed to compare online learning with instruction in traditional classrooms. While its focus was primarily on K-12 instruction it did provoke another study by Clary and Waldersee (2009). The focus of their inquiry was whether online education could provide an effective learning environment for teachers? Using anonymous surveys in individual online courses, they gathered teachers' opinions on whether online classrooms provided opportunities for successful professional development.

Online professional development allows teachers to receive training in a time that suits them, without having to leave the home, and most obviously can be specific to what an individual teacher wants to learn. Some of the earliest and still most common online professional development involved the teacher sitting at a computer with content delivered in a series of self-guided slides. Sawchuk (2009) describes a model of online professional development that has much promise. The "facilitated" format gives teachers access to certain materials, such as readings, which they read and complete related assignments on and take part in threaded discussions. The format allows for teachers to go back to their classrooms and attempt a new strategy and then connect with peers and facilitators to talk about what worked and what didn't.

There are still substantial challenges with online professional development, including finding ways to create online professional development that seems both compelling in its content and also more convenient, and easier to fit into the work life of a teacher rather than the face-to-face courses.

Implementing a new writing strategy requires more than just a traditional training model. This explored how effective the traditional model of training (one week face to face, with three face to face follow-up sessions) is with implementing a new writing strategy. It allows for experimenting with some online support structures that will hopefully enhance successful implementation as we continue to train new teachers.

A Work of A.R.T.
Accountability, Responsibility & Teamwork

The Vision and Responsibility

We might assume that every school or school district is a unified entity sharing a common goal. The School Superintendent surely wants the Principals to be instructional leaders who, in turn, expect the teachers to have the skills and the crafts for top quality teaching and are, therefore, capable of working closely with the parents who clearly want the best education for their children who have learned from their parents the value and joy of school learning.

Perhaps you think there's a touch of sarcasm or maybe just wishful thinking for the above expectation. Yet, we know there are a limited number of schools that achieve or almost achieve the above ideal. Most of these schools, we admit, are private or have economically advantaged students whose parents have a powerful voice or the option of moving their children to another school. With this economic division in our country, poor vs. middle or upper, native-born vs. immigrant, white vs. color, can we hope to assume that every school is capable of having this shared vision?

As we wrote in our previous chapters and attached lessons and ideas through the newly found power of technology, we kept making the pitch for the best possible educational strategies that would encompass all, or at least most, students with no withholding because of socio-economic status. If this equality is only a dream, then we are obligated to make this dream come true unless rich and middle class students remain the only beneficiaries of education and the "others" stay locked into poverty and raise their children to be caught in the same tragic destiny.

So in this chapter we're going to focus first on the PRINCIPAL. The Superintendent counts and must be held accountable by the community who depends on this person for hiring top quality principals, but it is the PRINCIPAL who is the prime caretaker of the school.

The Role of Elementary and Secondary School Principals

Principals are responsible for the overall operation of their schools which are often delineated. States and school districts have also set expectations for principals through their **principal evaluation criteria and procedures**. During the latter part of the twentieth century, as schools began to be held more accountable for the performance of their students on national and state assessments...they became more **responsible for teaching and learning in their schools**....With this change in responsibilities, principals discovered the need to **more effectively evaluate instruction** and **assist teachers as they worked to improve their instructional techniques.**

With schools facing increased pressure to improve teaching and learning, the duties and responsibilities of principals expanded further to **include the responsibility for leading school reform that would raise student achievement**. And often hinged upon a principal's ability to **create a shared vision within the school community** and in implementing new organizational structures that **engage teachers in shared decision-making.**

Principals are also **responsible for facilitating their school's interactions with parents and others in the school community**...which includes working with parents when disciplinary issues arise, when students are not succeeding academically, and when parents have concerns. Principals also interact with parents who serve on school advisory boards, parent/teacher organizations, and booster clubs.

We cite two standards from Guidelines *for Performance-Based Principal Evaluation, Missouri Department of Elementary and Secondary Education, 2003.* http://dese.mo.gov/divteachqual/leadership/profdev/PBPE.pdf (retrieved 12/30/13), http://dese.mo.gov/divteachqual/leadership/profdev/PBPE.pdf (retrieved 12/30/13)

What criteria related to principal behavior result in significant positive change?

Standard 1: A school administrator is an educational leader who promotes the success of all students by facilitating the development, articulation, implementation, and stewardship of a vision of learning that is shared and supported by the school community. The effective principal:

1.1 Uses research about best professional practice.

1.2 Recognizes the uniqueness and educability of each learner in a pluralistic society.

1.3 Plans for continuous, comprehensive, systemic school improvement.

1.4 Uses data for vision-driven change.

1.5 Promotes personal reflection (open to continuous review and revision through thoughtful study of one's beliefs and practices).

1.6 Uses fundamental principles of interpersonal communication, consensus building, conflict resolution, and organization change

Standard 2: A school administrator is an educational leader who promotes the success of all students by advocating, nurturing, and sustaining a school culture and instructional program conducive to student learning and staff professional growth. The effective principal:

2.1 Identifies and codifies varied instructional strategies.

2.2 Supports a culture for a caring school community.

2.3 Uses student assessment grounded in the belief that each student can learn.

2.4 Uses student data that improve instruction.

2.5 Develops, evaluates, and refines curriculum.

2.6 Plans professional development for staff.

2.7 Assesses the level of commitment to life-long learning of staff and students.

2.8 Assesses the nature of a school's climate and culture.

To the above standards, we want to add: A Principal must have a VISION of her/his school as a FOUNT OF LEARNING AND KNOWLEDGE which, through its staff and teaching style and strategies, impels students to come to the school every day with high expectations for having a WONDERFUL, MEANINGFUL day. But before a vision can be shared with a faculty, the first task a principal must do is help all the stakeholders understand and define what the current reality of their school is. This requires a set of inter-personal skills that many principals struggle with because it requires helping teachers see that current practice may not be sufficient to produce excellence. The administrators who have the relational skills to manage not only to their teachers but out to the parents and community, and up to the district administration, have the most success in creating on-going transformational change that lasts in their schools. Defining reality sets the stage for sharing and building vision in a school. Only then can the principal assume the role and perform the work of the school's educational leader.

To achieve the above standards, which we believe can be the backdrop for creating excellent schools; we would like to add our own "recipe" for the implementation and enhancement of these "rubrics" for Principals.

These are some of our requests. A principal should:

- spend more time in the classrooms and halls than in the office

- greet students by name as often as possible

- meet individually or in small groups with students who have shown various aspects of POSITIVE BEHAVIOR, so that going to the "Principals' Office" can be an honor

- should do at least one EXCITING, ENGAGING lesson every day (or at least three times a week) in different classrooms

- participate with the teachers and students in MAKING THE WALLS TALK with student work and accomplishments

- meet with small groups of teachers in COLLABORATIVE PLANNING AND EXCHANGE

- PARTICIPATE in staff development sessions

- SIT IN ON DEMONSTRATION LESSONS given by consultants and instructional coaches and discuss the effect of these lessons on student change and their learning

- To Principals and Teachers: Add your own requests

The Role of Teachers

We probably already know the role of teachers. Simply stated: *Be a good teacher and be fair to all your students.* Yet today, teachers are bearing the brunt of criticism for failing schools and low achievement. Teacher unions are criticized for *protecting* poor teachers and accepting low-quality teachers. The public schools (in contrast to the Charter and Private Schools) are blamed for accepting ineffective teaching and teachers who are often held responsible for the "achievement gap," the "high-dropout rate," "school violence", and whatever school problems exist. Yes, there are some teachers who need to improve, but then in every school the four of us have worked in or consulted in, we have met dedicated, hard-working teachers, eager to make their students succeed.

So in addition to the suggestions and activities we have presented as models for quality and engaging teaching, we want to offer suggestions and activities to the Principals, in the role of "Head Teachers".

Many of these suggestions will in many ways be similar to what we have proposed for students in the previous chapters. We hope—really hope—that you, Principals, will try them. Start by creating a Taxonomy of Your Teacher's Talents and Interests as illustrated in Figure 5.1. Start this at the opening of school and post and circulate this Taxonomy immediately so all the teachers have a resource from their peers. At an early faculty meeting have the teachers meet in interest groups and share their knowledge based on their interests and offer themselves as resources. Here's a sample Taxonomy that can come from any level school.

Figure 5.1 Teachers, Grades/ Subjects, Interests and Talents in a Middle School

TEACHER	GRADE(S)/SUBJECT(S)	INTERESTS AND TALENTS
Adams	Spanish, 7 & 8	football
Bono	Art	travel
Chang	Physical Education, Mandarin	dog breeding
Diaz	ESL	magic tricks
Eisen	Language Arts	interior design
Fruchter	Mathematics	baseball
Gavron	Physics	Shakespeare
Hermani	Drama	cross country
Irving	Music	jazz
Julio	Biology	mountain climbing
Kerry	Special Education	rock collecting
Larowitz	Health Education	comics
Maisano	Italian	baking
Marini	Film	organic gardening
Nguyen	Social Studies	storytelling
Olsen	Shop	ancestry
Petrovich	Career Education	golf
Quentin	English	singing
Rothstein	Independent Studies	ethnic cooking
Singh	Physics	rugby
Terranova	Computer Science	clarinet
Ungerleider	Geography	computer games
Vahdani	Global Studies	jogging
Williams	Ancient History	quilting
Xavier	Finance	swimming
Yamoto	Travel and Tourism	photography
Zucker	French	calligraphy

As we look at above figure, we see that a school is very likely to have a cadre of talents and knowledge. Yet as we generally assign each teacher to his or her classroom and allow limited time for collaboration, these wonderful talents remain obscured. Faculty meetings generally conducted by the Principal, deal with bureaucratic issues and frequently bypass the events of the classroom. The excuse of "no time" often allows for this neglect of classroom needs. As has been demonstrated in Finland, collaboration as been the engine for success and in Figure 5.2 we illustrate four different collaboration models which can be adapted to fit the culture of the individual school.

Figure 5.2 – Four Teacher Collaboration Models Presented by Teacher Participants at Teacher Faculty Meetings

COLLABORATION MODELS	ONE EXAMPLE OF FOCUS ON COLLABORATION	EXAMPLE OF ADDITONAL FOCUS	DISCUSSION AT FACULTY MEETING
Co-Teaching High school or middle school history and English teachers co-teach classes that combine their subject matter into a course called American Studies	Teachers meet regularly to discuss instructional issues	Monitor student progress. Discuss specific student needs	Different co-teacher groups compare plans, share activities, discuss student needs and progress
Station Teaching Teachers divide the content to be delivered and each takes responsibility for part of it. Some of the students may be completing independent work assignments or participating in peer tutoring. Each teacher instructs each part of the class, the equal status of sstudents and teachers is maximized.	Some of the students may be completing independent work assignments or participating in peer tutoring. Students benefit from the lower teacher-pupil ratio, and students with disabilities may be integrated into a group instead of being singled out.	Each teacher instructs each part of the class, the equal status of both students and teachers is maximized.	Teachers present how content is divided and how equal work and roles are maintained.

Parallel Teaching The teachers plan the instruction jointly, but each delivers it to half of the class group.	Requires that the teachers coordinate their efforts so that the students receive essentially the same instruction.	Appropriate for practice activities, projects needing close teacher supervision, and test review.	Teachers present "artifacts" of student work and test results.
Alternative Teaching Teachers share the instruction of students. The teachers may take turns leading a discussion, one may speak while the other demonstrates a concept, one may speak while the other models note taking on the chalkboard, and so on.	Teachers may role play, simulate conflict, and model appropriate question asking.	Fosters high level of mutual trust and inter-personal teacher commitment.	Teachers discuss rewards of this collaboration and also needs for effectiveness.

Who is a "Good" Teacher?

In the film *Waiting for Superman* (www.waiting for superman.com) the blame for failing schools is attributed to ineffective teachers and the teachers' unions that support and defend these poor teachers. In our opinion this general blame on teachers and teacher unions is a sad scapegoating that can only diminish the population of people choosing teaching as a career and will certainly reduce the number of teachers (of any quality) willing to teach in communities where there is low achievement. We want to define our own perception of what is a good teacher and suggest that all of you reading this book do the same, whether you are a teacher, administrator, parent, or citizen who deeply and desperately wants quality education for all our children—no exceptions. You're welcome to agree, disagree, and add your own. Following is Figure 5.3 *Qualities and Attributes of a "Good" Teacher.*

Figure 5.3 Qualities and Attributes of a "Good" Teacher

Among the qualities and attributes of being a good teacher:

1. Knows and understands the developmental stages and behaviors of children and/or adolescents

2. Loves to learn many subjects, ideas, stories, facts and whatever else is available to learn

3. Has a sense of humor and shares it with students

4. Is patient with student learning, but firm about what is important to learn

5. Knows the student' strengths, interests, and needs

6. Brings knowledge to the students from many sources

7. Is empathetic to student problems and difficulties

8. Shares her/his knowledge with the students freely and engagingly

9. Is aware of boredom and shuns it

10. Brings drama to learning

CHAPTER FIVE SHARED VISION & COMMITMENT BY ALL STAKEHOLDERS

> 11. Dialogues daily with students about what they have learned, understood, and will remember
>
> 12. Searches out with colleagues ideas and teaching behaviors that motivate students to learn
>
> 13. Generously praises student knowledge, creativity, engagement, empathy, diligence, sharing, and other worthy attributes
>
> 14. Remembers her/his own school days and relates this memory to the current students
>
> 15. Keeps working to get better and better and better

Not Enough Time

Many teachers feel they are under great pressure to "cover" their assigned curriculum and are deprived of the time they need to individualize or work with small groups or just have some fun. In fact, many charter schools today, freed of restrictions, have lengthened the school day, and even kindergarten children are being kept in school from 7:30 to 3 or 3:30 and are not allowed to nap any time during this marathon day! So in Figure 5.4 we present our suggestions for *SIX HOURS OF INSTRUCTION IN A FIVE HOUR DAY*. We're tried it ourselves, convinced other teachers, and have seen not only the instructional and learning benefits, but the student joy that comes from a meaningful and engaging school day. Here it is.

Figure 5.4 SIX HOURS OF INSTRUCTION IN A FIVE HOUR DAY.

Many students lose instructional time because of schedules and interruptions. They lose learning time before dismissal, before and after lunch, or between activities. During these and other non-instructional times we offer the following suggestions. Then add others and share them with colleagues.

- As students come into the room, play classical or semi-classical music (Beethoven, Mozart,Tchaikovsky) or any of your favorites or student favorites. Arrange for music monitors to find this music on the Internet or from available CD's. List the item on the board or SmartBoard. Have books, stories, or articles about the music or composers on a table, available for browsing.

- Have student writing of the previous day or week on a table with a large poster that says, WRITERS IN SEARCH OF ILLUSTRATORS. Provide instructions such as: "Choose a classmate's sentence or story and draw a picture or pictures for your choice. Be sure to read the writing carefully so that your illustrations match the writing."

- Post a unique mathematics problem for students to solve and illustrate. Offer extra credit or other reward to students who solve the problem.

- Ask students to become skilled etymologists and each day search the Internet for words with interesting stories. Students who do this activity can then meet with other students for "guessing" the story or just hearing it.

- Post student birthdays. Have the students make birthday cards during the "spare" time and give them to the "birthday student."

- Suggest that when a students find they "have nothing to do", they write a letter (by hand or computer) to:

    a) the principal telling about a great class activity

    b) another classmate telling of an important idea or some new learning

    c) a famous or newsworthy person telling of their admiration for her/his work or accomplishment

The Role of Parents & Caregiver

The role of the parents/caregiver is a touchy subject. All of us know that overburdened parents (whatever the term evokes) cannot have the same involvement as less burdened parents. Worrying about money, having limited knowledge of English, raising children without family help, working excessive hours are serious obstacles to school participation and create what we euphemistically call the Achievement Gap and Differentiation. So what can be done? We believe the place to begin is the classroom, with the assistance and agreement of the principal.

Schools can get parents involved more easily when parents see themselves having a positive role in the school life of their child. For example, parents are more likely to make a strong effort to come to school when their child is in a school performance in contrast to having a meeting with the teacher about their child's poor academic performance. A display of their children's art work or projects can bring reluctant parents to school. Sports activities are "parent popular." And a spaghetti dinner (or other ethnic food) put together with parent assistance has a better chance of bringing high attendance compared to a PTA meeting.

These aspects of parent involvement give the children a sense of the relationship between home and school and begin the building of a school community. And in a culturally responsive environment, the parents need to see—on the walls and in the classrooms--the cultural activities that we have been suggesting throughout this book.

The Role of the Students & ALL Self-Directed Learners

Students are supposed to know their roles: pay attention to the teacher, do your homework, cooperate in the classroom, be a good citizen. Signs in almost every classroom provide the rules or "roles" for the students. However, once in the classroom, the students are under the guidance or direction of the teacher and the teacher's influence. This *guidance* is not always easy, especially in culturally diverse environments when we are asking every child to "pay attention" and "conform."

So one of our primary recommendations is to give all the students a sense of their own potential and accomplishments. We start by proposing that in every classroom, from second grade and up, teachers have students frequently and consistently write Autobiographies and Memoirs that they share with the family members. Just share and share.

In Figures 5.5 to 5.12 we offer Writing Frames that can get your students started to share in the classroom, in the school, and in the home. The Writing Frames can be put on Youtube or other films, written in beautiful fonts, illustrated, and given as *gifts* to the parents or extended family. And family members are very likely to put aside their burdens when they are invited to watch and hear their children present in the classroom, assembly, stage, or any other public forum. We hope you try these and then add your own.

Figure 5.5 Looking Back

I am now _____ years old and I can remember many important events.
I remember the first time I _____
Then I remember when _____
When I was _____ years old, I _____
This year when I started _____ grade, I _____
I am now _____ years old and I can remember many important events.
I remember the first time I _____
Then I remember when _____
When I was _____ years old, I _____
This year when I started _____ grade, I _____

Figure 5.6 Memory Highlights

My life has had many events from the time I was born until now. Here are some highlights I would like to share.
First, there were my early years, from my birth till I went to school. (Write at least three events). _____
_____
_____
When I started school, there were many changes in my life.
_____
_____
_____
I also have memories of my family and family life.
_____
_____
_____

Figure 5.7 – Down Memory Lane

Think back to important events in your life and complete each sentence. Then add the details of that memory to the sentence.

One of my earliest memories is
_____(add details)
One of my happiest memories is
_____(add details)
One of my most exciting memories is
_____(add details)
In addition, I have several other memories I would like to share.
_____(add details

Figure 5.8 My Accomplishments From Then to Now

Although I am only _____ years old, I can look back on many accomplishments in my life.
When I was a preschooler, I already knew how to _____, _____, and _____.
By the time I entered school, I could _____, _____, and _____.
During my early school years, I _____, _____, and _____.
At this time of my life, I can _____, _____, and _____.
Having accomplished so much already, I know that I will be capable of _____, _____, and _____.

Figure 5. 9 Feelings

Like all people, I have many feelings, some pleasant and some unpleasant. Here are some of my feelings I would like to share. I laugh when _____ I get angry when _____ I feel great when _____ I worry when _____ I feel I have had a great day when _____

Figure 5.10 If I Could….

Write three or four more sentences telling what you would do to make what you would like to do to make theses dreams happen.

If I could do one great act in my life, I _____ If I could honor a wonderful person, I _____ If I could travel to any place I wanted, I _____ If I could help people in need, I _____ If I good entertain one person of accomplishment, I _____

Figure 5.11 I Have a Dream

Use this Frame based on the model of Dr. Martin Luther King, Jr. to write your dream of the future. Your dream might be about your personal life or how you might help others. Add details to each starting sentence.

```
I have a dream that _____
In this dream, I see myself _____
To make this dream come true I _____
```

Figure 5.12 Ten Years From Now

Imagine yourself ten years from now. Complete the frame and add details. .

```
Ten years from now, I will be _____ years old.
I expect to have _____
I might be living _____
Hopefully, I will be planning _____
As I look ahead to the future, I know that
_____
```

Defining Learning

Teachers must be engaged in continuously defining what students must learn. In our current world of high-stakes testing, we can be side-tracked about what students not only need to learn, but are motivated to learn. The strongest motivator or student engagement and learning is confidence in the ability to understand what is being taught and to express that confidence. Figure 5.12 is an example of "I Can" statements from a science class.

Figure 5.12 "I Can..." Here is an example of *"I Can...."* statements that will help you remember facts and ideas you need to know about any topic or subject you are studying.

I can justify the importance of photosynthesis by citing the follow three ideas or concepts:

    First, _____

    Following that, _____

    Finally _____

I can distinguish a physical property from a chemical property in three ways.

First in importance is _____

After that, _____

Then _____

I can list at least three list properties I would use to classify a substance. These properties are (1)_____(2)_____.and (3)_____

Epilogue: The Future of the 21st Century - What is the Vision?

Each generation has struggled with the concept of the future. Will our children's lives be better than in previous generations, with less disease and less poverty? Will they grow up in a safer, more peaceful world? Will they have sustaining jobs and lives with good relationships? And how will the onslaught of inventions that have always been the hallmark of human development affect—in positive ways—the world our children and grandchildren will have to live in?

Because crystal balls are not dependable, we have to speculate from what we already have and then predict. And today, we are already beyond the brink of what we call the Technology of the Digital Evolution. So our vision is that, if all goes well, the Digital World, with its growing potential of making global communication a daily possibility, can also make our Cultural Universals the unifier of our lives. If we agree that all cultures want the best for their children—however they see it—we can use the technological starting points already available and improving at *nano-speed*. Here are some of the already existing unifiers:

- *Rapid translations of languages across the world.* A Chinese speaker can quickly communicate with a Spanish speaker.

- *Instant visualizations.* We can travel through the streets of Paris or Singapore or Bethlehem or any other place, finding our way, hearing its sounds, and maybe (who knows?) inhaling the aromas of delicious foods.

- *Understanding our differences and similarities.* Why do we dress as we do? Eat as we do? Pray or not pray as we do? Celebrate as we do? Through voice and visualizations and direct communication, we have new chances to "getting to know you." We are likely to hate less if we know more.

- *Sharing our knowledge world-wide.* All of us who have had the experience of traveling "abroad" or meeting "new" people know the exhilaration of these encounters. We come back better educated and hopefully wiser or gentler or kinder. The digital world can give us some of these experiences as starters and the incentives to check out the realities.

These are just a few of the possibilities. We know you have your own. And now, to define excellence, and to make that excellence a reality, we have to lay the groundwork of culturally responsive classrooms. We hope the ideas and activities in this book and its additional materials help add to your plans for making all of your students fully prepared for this century and its potential.

Excellence in a culturally responsive model means ALL the students learn it. So assessment tells us if the student did or did not learn it, the most important component of this entire process is to be able to, as professional educators, answer what we will do when a student doesn't learn. When we have a system built into our school structure that provides the re-teaching, intervention and support so that ALL students learn, then we are excellent.

REFERENCES

Bandura, A. (1997). *Self-efficacy: The exercise of control*. New York: W.H. Freeman.

Bandura, A. (1986). *Social foundations of thought and action*. Englewood Cliffs, NJ: Prentice-Hall.

Bandura, A. (1973). *Aggression: A social learning analysis*. Englewood Cliffs, NJ: Prentice-Hall.

Bandura, A. (1977). *Social learning theory*. New York: General Learning Press.

Bandura, A. (1969). *Principles of behavior modification*. New York: Holt, Rinehart & Winston.

Bandura, A. & Walters, R. (1963). *Social learning and personality development*. New York: Holt, Rinehart & Winston.

Brooks, J. and Brooks, M. (1999) *The case for constructivist classrooms*. New York: Prentice Hall.

Brown, J.S., Collins, A. & Duguid, S. (1989). *Situated cognition and the culture of learning*. Educational Researcher, 18(1), 32-42.

Carroll, Lewis. (1965).. *Alice in Wonderland* New York: Random House (originally published 1871).

Crystal, D. (1995). The Cambridge encyclopedia of the English language. 2nd ed). New York: Cambridge University Press.

Delpit, L. (2001). The skin that we speak. New York: The New Press.

Diamond, J. (1999) *Guns, germs, and steel*. New York: W.W. Norton & Co.

Feuerstein, R. Rand, Y. Falik, L, & Feuerstein, R. (2006). Feuerstein instrumental enrichment program . London: Routledge Books.
Dynamic Assessment of Cognitive Modifiability by Reuven Feuerstein, Y. Rand, L. Falik & Ra. S. Feuerstein,2003.

Feuerstein's Theory and Applied Systems: A Reader by Reuven Feuerstein et al., 2003.

Futernick, K. (2007). A possible dream: Retaining California teachers so all students learn. Sacramento: California State University.

Gay. G. (2000). *Culturally responsive teaching: theory, research, & practice.* New York: Teachers College Press.

Gardner, H. (1993*). Multiple intelligences.* New York: Basic Books.
Gardner, H. (1983*). Frames of the Mind.* New York: Basic Books.
Gay. G. (2000). *Culturally responsive teaching: theory, research, & practice.* New York: Teachers College Press.

Goddard, Y. L., Goddard, R. D., Tschannen-Moran, M. (2007). *A theoretical and empirical investigation of teacher collaboration for school improvement and student achievement in public elementary schools.* Teachers College Record, 109(4), 877-896.

Guarino, C. M., Santibanez, L., & Daley, G. A. (2006). *Teacher recruitment and retention: A review of the recent empirical literature.* Review of Educational Research, 76(2), 173-208.

Hamby, J. V. (1989). *How to get an "A" on your dropout prevention report card. Educational Leadership, 46* (5), 21-28.

Herman, R., Dawson, P., Dee, T., Greene, J., Maynard, R., Redding, S., & Darwin, M. (2008*). Turning around chronically low-performing schools: A practice guide* (NCEE #2008-4020). Washington, D.C.: U.S. Department of Education, Institute of Education Sciences, National Center for Education Evaluation and Regional Assistance.

Kardos, S. M., & Johnson, S. M. (2007). On their own and presumed expert: New teachers' experience with their colleagues. Teachers College Record, 109(9), 2083-2106.
Hyerle, D. (1995). *Thinking maps: tools for learning.* Cary, NC: Innovative Science.
Juster, N (1989). *The phantom tollbooth.* New York. Random House.

Lave, J. (1988). *Cognition in practice: Mind, mathematics, and culture in everyday life.* Cambridge, UK: Cambridge University Press.

Lave, J., & Wenger, E. (1990). *Situated learning: legitimate peripheral participation.* Cambridge, UK: Cambridge University Press.

LeVine, Robert A. and Merry I. White. (1986) *The cultural basis of educational development.* New York: Routledge and Kegan.

Maisano, M., and Olsen, R. (2010). Second life: A technological simulation for culturally responsive teaching for every classroom. *American Journal of Educational Studies,* 1(3), 52, 121-129.

McLellan, H. (1995*). Situated Learning Perspectives*. Englewood Cliffs, NJ: Educational Technology Publi)

Prensky, M. (2010). *Digital natives: partnering for real learning.* Thousand Oaks, Ca. Corwin Press.

Primack, E & Abrams, N.E. (2006). *The view from the center of the universe.* . New York: Riverhead Books.

Rabbit Proof Fence (film 2002). *Wikipedia,* 2009.

Rothstein, A, Rothstein, E, & Lauber, G. (2007) *Writing as learning.* Thousand Oaks, CA: Corwin Press.

Rothstein, A, Rothstein, E, & Lauber, G. (2007) *Write for mathematics.* Thousand Oaks, CA: Corwin Press.

Rothstein, E. & Rothstein, A. (2009) *English Grammar Instruction That Works*. Thousand Oaks, CA: Corwin Press.

Sobol, D. (1999). (1999) *Galileo's daughter.* New York: The Penguin Group.

www.ingramcontent.com/pod-product-compliance
Lightning Source LLC
Chambersburg PA
CBHW081208170426
43198CB00018B/2895